Resurrection Power

RESURRECTION POWER!

50 Days That Rocked The World.

A Devotional Journey.

Copyright © 2014 by Rob Still

All rights reserved.

Resurrection Power. 50 Days That Rocked The World. A Devotional Journey.

All rights reserved under International and Pan-American Copyright Conventions. By payment of the required fees, you have been granted the non-exclusive, non-transferable right to access and read the text of this e-book on-screen. No part of this text may be reproduced, transmitted, downloaded, decompiled, reverse engineered, or stored in or introduced into any information storage and retrieval system, in any form or by any means, whether electronic or mechanical, now known or hereinafter invented, without the express written permission of Wholehearted Worship Worldwide, a dba of Still Music Group Inc, & Rob Still.

ePub Edition 2014 Requests for information should be addressed to: Wholehearted Worship Worldwide a dba of Still Music Group Inc, & Rob Still, Nashville, Tennessee 37013

Library of Congress Cataloging-in-Publication Data
Resurrection Power. 50 Days That Rocked The World. A Devotional Journey/Robert M. Still, Jr.

Still, Rob Resurrection Power. 50 Days That Rocked The World. A Devotional Journey (Kindle Locations _-_).Publishing Co. Kindle Edition.

Printed in the United States of America

Contents

Introduction: Why I Wrote This Book		1
1.	Now What? An Easter Season Devotional	3
2.	Resurrection Power	7
3.	Set Your Heart	11
4.	Many a Doubt	13
5.	"My Lord and My God!"	17
6.	All Things New	21
7.	Church of the Burning Hearts	25
8.	Building A Relational History	29
9.	Remember You've Been Raised From The Dead!	33
10.	Resurrection of A Dream	37
11.	Feed My Sheep	41
12.	A Servant Leader Movement	45
13.	Conspiracy Theory	49
14.	Do This To Remember	53
15.	Truth or Lie?	57
16.	Moses and the Prophets	61
17.	What Is That To You?	65
18.	Dressed in White	69
19.	Peace Be With You	73
20.	Ghost Busters	77
21.	Wait Until	81
22.	The Power of An Opened Mind	85
23.	Proclaim Repentance and Forgiveness	89
24.	To All Nations	93
25.	Why Jerusalem?	97
26.	The Power of Witness	101
27.	What Are You Waiting For?	105
28.	We Gather Together	109
29.	What Did He Promise?	113
30.	Power From On High	117
31.	Just As He Told You	121
32.	500 Witnesses	125
33.	Preparing For Transition	129
34.	Rest and Recreation	133

35.	Seven Sundays of Easter	137
36.	Tribe of The Like-Minded	141
37.	Worship and Doubt	145
38.	All Authority	149
39.	He Ascended Into Heaven	153
40.	He's Coming Back!	157
41.	Timing Is God's Business	161
42.	From Tribe to Family	165
43.	Living Water!	169
44.	How God Chooses Leaders	173
45.	Lo, I Am With You Always	177
46.	Signs, Wonders, and Miracles	181
47.	Pour Out Your Spirit Lord!	187
48.	Visions and Dreams	191
49.	The Significance of Pentecost	195
50.	Joy Is The Secret Sauce	199
51.	Epilogue: Where Do We Go From Here?	203

Bonus Resources	207
About The Author	209
Music By Rob Still	211
About Our Missions Work	213

Introduction: Why I Wrote This Book

A Devotional Series for the Easter Season

Most mornings I take a photograph of the sunrise and post it on Instagram/Twitter/Facebook with a devotional scripture or thought. On the Monday after Easter Sunday last year I felt prompted by the Holy Spirit to go deeper with this practice.

I made a video to explain the idea of launching a series of short devotionals on my blog exploring the spirituality of the season from *Easter to Pentecost*. You can see this *Devotional Series Video* on my Youtube channel (http://www.youtube.com/user/RobStillMusic).

According to the historical church calendar, the *Easter Season* (also known as *Easter Tide*) is the 50 day period from Resurrection Sunday to Pentecost Sunday. In this series we'll look at Jesus' final instructions to his disciples, the ascension, the coming of the Holy Spirit at Pentecost, what it means to develop a resurrection mentality … and whatever else I end up writing. 😄

It Takes A Season

I had the joy of sitting under the teaching of Dr. Robert E. Webber during my studies at the Institute for Worship Studies. In Chapter 7 "Easter" of his book *Ancient-Future Time: Forming Spirituality through the Christian Year* he says observing Easter is much more than a one day event.

"The primary metaphor for the Easter season is the church as the resurrected people living a resurrected spirituality. Because of Easter we are in union with Christ and are called to live in our baptismal identity in his resurrection. This essential theme of Easter cannot be communicated in a day. It takes a season." -Robert E. Webber, Ancient-Future Time (Grand Rapids: Baker Books, 2004), p. 148.

So in the spirit of discovery and living out loud, for this 50 day season I'll post a fresh devotional thought with my **sunrise photo** of that morning, everyday through Pentecost, commenting as the Spirit inspires. God has already been showing me a lot.

Let Us Pray

"Father, I want to know Christ, and the power of his resurrection living in me. Renew my mind and transform my personality, that I may give You glory in all I say and do. Thank you for the gift of a new life, and your resurrection power to walk in your ways, and do your will. In Jesus Holy name. Amen."

1

Now What? An Easter Season Devotional

Jesus said, "Peace be with you! As the Father has sent me, I am sending you." And with that he breathed on them and said, "Receive the Holy Spirit." John 20:21-22 [Sunrise photo April 1, 2013]

Day 1 – "Now What?"

Like the followers of Jesus immediately following his death, I have felt the overwhelming grief of loss a few times in my life. You probably have too, and if not yet, you will.

Death and loss are the parts of life that no one escapes.

But all loss is not the same. Losing a loved one to death is not the same as losing your job or moving to a new location. Still, all loss is painful – even when it is necessary for a greater good.

For some, the biggest losses have been the loss of a dream. I would put myself in that category, how about you?

Competitive athletes fall into this category. I like to watch sports, and you can see the disappointment on the face of the elite athlete who dedicates years of training for the purpose of winning some ultimate prize, only to fall short of the big dream.

So close and yet so far.

It hurts to lose. Yet, I'm a shameless idealist, and hopefully will remain one as long as I have breath.

In my life journey so far I have gained and lost several "dreams":

- my dream business in the music industry where I did meaningful work that supported many musicians and singers
- my dream recording studio where we could do full tracking and mix sessions at the highest level
- our beautiful 4000 sf dream home we designed and built on 15 secluded acres in Brentwood
- and later, my "dream job" at our beloved church of 26 years

Make your own list of losses that have impacted you. What emotions do you feel?

- Sadness.
- Shock.
- Grief.
- Despair.
- Dreams crushed.
- All hope gone.

And of course, death is the *ultimate ending.*

Game over.

You're done.

Whatever the loss, the emotions are similar.

It's not hard to imagine the overwhelming sense of loss those friends of Jesus felt on that Resurrection Sunday.

But then a miracle happened. Jesus showed up, alive and empowered.

> *"Peace I give you"*

What is peace? Peace is harmony, tranquility, security, and freedom from fear. It means the end of strife and contention. Peace is good, and it is for peace that the human spirit is designed.

The peace of God is what our souls long for. This was the first gift Jesus gave his grieving disciples. And this is the gift He gives you and me in our moments of despair. Peace is healing for the wounded soul.

He gives us *beauty for ashes, and joy for mourning.* (Isaiah 61:3)

> **"As the the Father sent Me, I am now sending you."**

Jesus' next words give hope for a meaningful future. "I am sending you." You and I have a mission, to be sent as Jesus was sent. Jesus was sent to bring healing and reconciliation, to establish the Kingdom of God. This is the mission he gives to us, to be his representatives in this natural world.

"He breathed on them. Receive the Holy Spirit."

Jesus had supernatural power. He now bestows that source of power on his followers. When we receive the Holy Spirit, our lives are in agreement with His truth.

> *"Christ in me, the hope of glory." Colossians 1:26*
>
> *"I can do all things through Christ Jesus who gives me strength." Philippians 4:13*

By receiving the Holy Spirit, we are empowered as disciples of Jesus (*and sons and daughters of God!*) to carry on the mission of the gospel.

Let Us Pray

"Father, thank you for the gift of your peace. Now I receive the gift of Your Holy Spirit. I desire to be sent as Jesus was sent, to bring glory to your name. Amen."

2

Resurrection Power

"The Spirit of God, who raised Jesus from the dead, lives in you. And just as God raised Christ Jesus from the dead, he will give life to your mortal bodies by this same Spirit living within you." Romans 8:11 [Sunrise photo April 2, 2013]

Day 2 Resurrection Power

> *Death cannot keep its prey, Jesus my Savior;*
> *he tore the bars away, Jesus my Lord!*
>
> *Up from the grave he arose;*
> *with a mighty triumph o'er his foes;*
> *he arose a victor from the dark domain,*
> *and he lives forever, with his saints to reign.*
> *He arose! He arose!*
>
> *Hallelujah! Christ arose!*
> Up From The Grave – Robert Lowry, 1826-1899

Jesus coming back from the dead is THE game changer. The whole Christian faith is based on this central fact.

What does that mean for you and me? *Everything.*

For starters, **nothing is impossible.**

This is the power of God available for us. *"Everything is possible to one who believes."* Mark 9:23

Meditate on this truth. His resurrection power rescued all creation, and it will transform your life.

Let faith rise up! The power that raised Jesus from the grave will accomplish the purposes of God in your life.

Romans 8:11 articulates this promise of God to redirect our destiny, the way we live in the here and now – from death to life:

> "But for you who welcome him, in whom he dwells—even though you still experience all the limitations of sin—you yourself experience life on God's terms. It stands to reason, doesn't it, that if the alive-and-present God who raised

Jesus from the dead moves into your life, **he'll do the same thing in you that he did in Jesus**, bringing you alive to himself? When God lives and breathes in you (and he does, as surely as he did in Jesus), you are delivered from that dead life. **With his Spirit living in you, your body will be as alive as Christ's!**" Romans 8:11 (The Message)

There is power, power,
wonder working power
in the precious blood of the Lamb.
"Power in The Blood"- Words & Music: Lewis E. Jones, 1899

Let Us Pray

"God fill me today with your Spirit, the Spirit that raised Jesus from the dead. Fulfill your purposes for me today. In Jesus name. Amen."

3

Set Your Heart

Since you have been raised with Christ, set your hearts on things above, where Christ is seated at the right hand of God. Colossians 3:1 [Sunrise Pic April 3 2013]

Day 3 Where Is Your Heart Set?

In Colossians 3 apostle Paul describes what it means to be a resurrected person – *"since you have been raised with Christ"*. If Jesus is truly Lord of your life, you are now a different person, with a new identity and a new mission.

"... set your heart on things above". Now you have a new focus and holy purpose. To do the will of God.

"where Christ is seated at the right hand of God" This is royalty imagery. It means Jesus has the highest authority. He is our advocate before the King of the Universe.

His agenda? *"May Your Kingdom come, and Your will be done, on earth as it is in heaven."*

Let Us Pray

"God help me set my heart, my emotional energy, on things above. Show me Your heart's desires and Your will. Make me an instrument of Your peace . Thank you that Jesus is sitting at the right hand of the Father, and He is making intercession for us to walk in the fullness of your purposes. Thank you Lord. In the name of the Father, Son and Holy Spirit. Amen."

4

Many a Doubt

Then Jesus told him, "Because you have seen me, you have believed; blessed are those who have not seen and yet have believed." John 20:29 [Sunrise photo April 4, 2013]

Day 4 Many A Doubt

Just as I am, though tossed about
with many a conflict, many a doubt,
fightings and fears within, without,
O Lamb of God, I come, I come.

Just As I Am text by Charlotte Elliott, 1789-1871, new music by Rob Still, available on **iTunes**

Faith is simple, but not easy.

I hear lots of people talk about having "faith", even "faith in God", but they're not talking about faith in the God of the Bible, the God of Abraham, Isaac and Jacob.

They're not talking having faith in the life, death and resurrection of Jesus Christ, but rather some vague hope that the "universe" will magically cause everything to work out OK.

That is not faith, that is wishful thinking.

Are You Skeptical?

"Doubting" Thomas was a guy who thought things through. He was committed to truth. He wanted the facts. This is the upside of critical thinking.

He was also brave, willing to follow Jesus to death – which he eventually did. When Jesus decided to put himself in imminent danger to minister the gospel, Thomas was the disciple who said *"Let us also go, so that we may die with Him."* (John 11:16)

"Skepticism", defined as *"doubt about the truth of something"* is a great thinking tool when your worldview is open to believing the unbelievable.

Ultimately we believe in the resurrection as an act of faith.

Thomas believed based on the facts.

Jesus Appears to Thomas

^{24} Now Thomas (also known as Didymus), one of the Twelve, was not with the disciples when Jesus came. ^{25} So the other disciples told him, "We have seen the Lord!"

But he said to them, "Unless I see the nail marks in his hands and put my finger where the nails were, and put my hand into his side, I will not believe."

^{26} A week later his disciples were in the house again, and Thomas was with them. Though the doors were locked, Jesus came and stood among them and said, "Peace be with you!"
^{27} Then he said to Thomas, "Put your finger here; see my hands. Reach out your hand and put it into my side. Stop doubting and believe."

^{28} Thomas said to him, "My Lord and my God!"

^{29} Then Jesus told him, "Because you have seen me, you have believed; blessed are those who have not seen and yet have believed." (John 20:24-29)

The invitation of our Savior is the same today as it was then.

Stop doubting and believe.

Let Us Pray

"God I want to believe. Help my unbelief. Give me courage to follow You, serve You, and walk in your ways today. Amen."

5

"My Lord and My God!"

The high point of faith is to acknowledge Jesus Christ as one's Lord and God. NIV commentary on John 20:28 [Sunrise Photo April 5 2013]

Day 5 "My Lord and My God!"

Thomas was convinced by the living, breathing, physical presence of Jesus appearing after his death and burial.

He must have witnessed the crucifixion. He would have watched his rabbi, his mentor, his coach – brutally die. He must have seen his Master's blood poured out.

There was no way Thomas could believe this "story" that *"He's alive"* was possibly true.

But the presence of Jesus changes everything.

Jesus invites Thomas to investigate for himself. He touches the nail scarred hands, and puts his hand in the wound on Christ's side.

Then Thomas was convinced. He had experienced a supernatural miracle. *Only God could do this*, and God was standing there in front of him.

His response was *worship*. *"Ego Kyrios kai ego Theos!"*

"My Lord and my God!"

Worship is a pattern of revelation and response.

The NIV commentary says of Thomas's response (John 20:28):

> *"To acknowledge Jesus as one's Lord and God is the high point of faith."*

What makes worship *Christian*? The centrality of Jesus Christ. Every time we worship, there is one primary truth that we are to remember and proclaim in some way.

Jesus is Lord!

Let Us Pray

"Jesus you are Lord of all. You are Lord of creation and Lord of my life. You are King of Kings and Lord of Lords. I ask for more revelation of who You really are. Help me boldly share the good news of your love and your kingdom. In the name of the Father, Son, and Holy Spirit. Amen."

6

All Things New

Behold I make all things new! Revelation 21:5 [Sunrise Photo April 6, 2013]

Day 6 All Things New

Strength for today and bright hope for tomorrow. Great Is Thy Faithfulness (Thomas Chisholm, 1866–1960)

The game changing truth about Easter?

God makes all things new.

When we choose to die with him, we are also raised with Him. It is a new beginning.

> "The biblical metaphor for Easter spirituality is found in baptism. The baptized life is a life that is lived in the pattern of death and resurrection." (Robert Webber *Ancient-Future Time: Forming Spirituality through the Christian Year* p.146)

Have you ever had times in your life when things were so mucked up you thought – "I just need to start over, with a clean slate"?

This is the power of Christ in you and me, "the hope of glory" (Colossians 1:27).

Through Christ, God empowers His children to overcome *all evil* – whether the flesh, the world or the devil (1 John 2:16-17).

Worship as a lifestyle.

We participate in worship as a lifestyle by living daily with the mindset of "dead to self, and alive in Christ" (Romans 6:11).

Worship is more than intellectual agreement with truth, as important as that is. Worship is more then feeling the presence of God and other emotions of being close with God, as important as that is.

Worship in this sense, is the daily, moment by moment experience where we choose in every situation to die to sin and live in the Spirit.

"When men renounce Satan and believe in God, when they pass from corruption to a new life, when they lay aside the image of the earthly man and take on the form of the heavenly Man, they go through a kind of death and resurrection." St Leo the Great

"Behold, I am making all things new." Revelation 21:5

The new creation life is a lifestyle of worship.

For the follower of Jesus, life will never be the same.

Let Us Pray

"Jesus thank you that I am a new creation. Thank you for the gift of a new beginning. Empower me today to live in agreement with your Spirit; dead to sin and self, but alive in Christ. For Your glory. In the name of the Father, Son and Holy Spirit. Amen."

7

Church of the Burning Hearts

"Were not our hearts burning?" Luke 24:32 [Sunrise photo April 7 2013]

Day 7 Church of the Burning Hearts

> *They said to each other, "Didn't our hearts burn within us as he talked with us on the road and explained the Scriptures to us?"* Luke 24:32

Scripture records twelve resurrection appearances of Jesus, the first six in Jerusalem, four in Galilee, one on the Mount of Olives, and one on the road to Damascus.

In the ancient church, the focus of the second Sunday of Easter is the church. Sermon topics on this day will often be on "Doubting Thomas", or "The Emmaus Road".

Why does the church even exist? Because of the resurrection.

> *The church is the community of God's people defined by the Easter event and called to live out the resurrected life.* ((Robert Webber *Ancient-Future Time: Forming Spirituality through the Christian Year* p. 149)

Luke chapter 24, verses 13 through 35 records the story known as *"On The Road to Emmaus"*. Take a minute to read it right now, then come back and read on.

Jesus was physically present, but He was not recognized.

The fact that Jesus was walking and talking to people who knew who He was, but they did not "see him" actually encourages me. Why? Because the revelation of Jesus was not in his physical presence, but in the effect he had on their spirits.

> *"Were not our hearts burning?"*

I can relate to the burning heart. That's how I felt at 12 years of age, led by the burn in my heart to walk forward one Sunday night in a little Baptist church in Salisbury, MD and give my life to Jesus.

John Wesley experienced the same thing at Aldersgate.

> *I felt my heart strangely warmed. I felt I did trust in Christ alone for salvation; and an assurance was given me that He had taken away **my** sins, even **mine**, and saved **me** from the law of sin and death.* The Journal of John Wesley, May 24, 1738

Faith in Jesus is more than perpetuating a religious and cultural institution. Faith is a matter of the heart, responding to the presence of Jesus.

Worship as burning hearts gathered together.

The first disciples and followers of Jesus gathered together because *their hearts were burning.* Jesus had taught them of His kingdom and had given them a mission to tell the good news.

They gathered to remember, encourage and act. They encouraged one another with "psalms, hymns and spiritual songs" (Colossians 3:16)

The truth of the resurrection transformed them from fearful and defeated into bold world changers.

They were supernaturally motivated. They did not take their cues from the culture around them to be "relevant", they were counter-culture.

They were the church of the burning hearts. That's the church Jesus invites us to join. That's the one I want to be part of.

Let Us Pray

"Jesus open the eyes of my heart, that I may see You as You really are. Fill me with zeal for your house. Bless your church with passion for Your kingdom to come, and Your will be done, on earth as it is in heaven. In the name of the Father, Son and Holy Spirit. Amen."

8

Building A Relational History

"Jesus also did many other things" John 21:25 [Sunrise photo April 8, 2013]

Day 8 Many Other Things

> *Jesus also did many other things. If they were all written down, I suppose the whole world could not contain the books that would be written.* John 21:25

The longer we walk with the Lord and build a relational history with Him, the more we realize we have a long way to go. I've heard many experts with decades of experience in a particular subject say something to the effect of , "the more I know, the more I realize I don't know."

When I began to "study to show thyself as one approved" (2 Timothy 3:15), one day I realized that the study of God, the "knowledge of God", is inexhaustible.

God is completely fascinating. If you're bored with this stuff, it's because you don't realize what you are lacking.

> *You don't realize that you are wretched and miserable and poor and blind and naked.* Revelation 3:17

People need God. It's a built-in design of the human spirit.

Jesus *revealed* God in the fullness of His reality, His truth. Jesus showed us who God really is and what God is really like.

How?

By His life and teaching, as well as His death and resurrection. During His 33 years on the earth, Jesus did much more than could be documented by men. He was supernaturally productive, demonstrating the love of God so that we might build up our faith in Him.

> *Jesus performed many other signs in the presence of his disciples, which are not recorded in this book. But these are written that you may believe that Jesus is the Messiah, the Son of*

God, and that by believing you may have life in his name. John 20:30-31

Worship is response to God's invitation.

Healthy relationships are built on mutual love, trust, respect and intimacy.

The invitation of God is to engage in a healthy relationship with Him.

"Get to know me" He seems to be saying, "because I already know everything about you. I desire to bless you, but you gotta do life my way. If you do that, you're gonna be a whole lot happier." (Uncle Robbie paraphrase).

It is a lifelong quest to build a spiritual history with God, to invest in an authentic, sincere relationship with Father, Son and Holy Spirit.

But the rewards are worth it. There is joy in the journey.

Let Us Pray

"Jesus thank you for showing me the Father. Thank you that You know me completely. Help me to know You more, moment by moment, day by day, chapter by chapter. By Your Spirit and for Your glory. Help me to do Your will today. In the name of the Father, Son and Holy Spirit. Amen."

9

Remember You've Been Raised From The Dead!

Throw yourselves wholeheartedly and full-time – remember, you've been raised from the dead! – into God's way of doing things. Romans 6:13 [Sunrise photo April 9, 2013]

Day 9 Remember You've Been Raised From The Dead!

*I am a new creation, born of the Spirit of God.
I have a destination, in the presence of my Father.*
What Words Can't Say (c) Rob Still Music

Followers of Jesus are resurrection people. "I was dead, but now I'm alive."

What if we really lived like we used to be dead, but now are alive?

I know some people who have had near death experiences, and it completely changed their outlook on life. What if we shifted our perspective to embrace the power of this invisible reality, the truth of resurrection power at work in our everyday lives?

Paul in Romans 6: 1-13 thoroughly explains this new-life reality.

3-5 That's what baptism into the life of Jesus means. When we are lowered into the water, it is like the burial of Jesus; when we are raised up out of the water, it is like the resurrection of Jesus. Each of us is raised into a light-filled world by our Father so that we can see where we're going in our new grace-sovereign country.

In worship we remember.

Through out scripture we are instructed to remember the Lord.

This is the subtitle of Deuteronomy 8 **"Remember the Lord Your God".**

This is the instruction Jesus gave at communion – "do this in remembrance of me" (Luke 22:19)

So too, as we face the war raging in our own lives, we need to remember the powerful truth that baptism symbolizes.

In baptism, we make a public declaration that we are part of the Jesus movement.

Jesus experienced humiliation and pain, enduring the consequences of our sin on our behalf. In a similar way, through baptism we humble ourselves, choosing to die with him in baptism, and rising with him in new life. Remember that!

> *When Martin Luther felt discouraged or afraid, he'd often splash water on himself and declare, "But I am baptized!" John Calvin advised readers depressed by evil to "reflect that they are still on the way" to the "complete victory" that God promises in baptism.* Calvin Worship Symposium

Today you are a new creation. Remember your baptism.

His mercies are new every morning.

Let Us Pray:

"Lord thank you for redeeming me. Help me remember that I was lost, but now I am found; I was dead, but now I am alive. I remember my baptism – I am dead to sin, and alive in Christ. Renew my mind today. In Jesus name, Amen."

Bonus Reading:

When Death Becomes Life Romans 6 – The Message

6 1-3 So what do we do? Keep on sinning so God can keep on forgiving? I should hope not! If we've left the country where sin is sovereign, how can we still live in our old house there? Or didn't you realize we packed up and left there for good? That is what happened in baptism. When we went under the water, we left the old country of sin behind; when we came up out of the water, we entered into the new country of grace—a new life in a new land!

3-5 That's what baptism into the life of Jesus means. When we are lowered into the water, it is like the burial of Jesus; when we are raised up out of the water, it is like the resurrection of Jesus. Each of us is raised into a light-filled world by our Father so that we can see where we're going in our new grace-sovereign country.

6-11 Could it be any clearer? Our old way of life was nailed to the cross with Christ, a decisive end to that sin-miserable life—no longer at sin's every beck and call! What we believe is this: If we get included in Christ's sin-conquering death, we also get included in his life-saving resurrection. We know that when Jesus was raised from the dead it was a signal of the end of death-as-the-end. Never again will death have the last word. When Jesus died, he took sin down with him, but alive he brings God down to us. From now on, think of it this way: Sin speaks a dead language that means nothing to you; God speaks your mother tongue, and you hang on every word. You are dead to sin and alive to God. That's what Jesus did.

12-14 That means you must not give sin a vote in the way you conduct your lives. Don't give it the time of day. Don't even run little errands that are connected with that old way of life. Throw yourselves wholeheartedly and full-time—remember, you've been raised from the dead!—into God's way of doing things. Sin can't tell you how to live. After all, you're not living under that old tyranny any longer. You're living in the freedom of God.

10

Resurrection of A Dream

"Follow Me, and I will make you fishers of men." Matthew 4:19 [Sunrise photo April 10, 2013]

Day 10 Death and Resurrection of A Dream

I'm going fishing!
Peter in John 21:3

The Bible documents twelve unique resurrection appearances of Jesus – six in Jerusalem, four in Galilee, one on the Mount of Olives, and one on the road to Damascus.

John 21 records the third appearance to the disciples after he was raised from the dead (John 21: 14) There are two primary stories in this chapter, "Jesus and the Miraculous Catch of Fish" and "Jesus Reinstates Peter".

Death of A Dream

For the disciples, it was all over. They were done.

The dream had died. The vision blown up. The mission melted down.

Not knowing how to move forward, Peter moved backward. Maybe he was thinking, "I'm going back to what I know."

His occupation had been fishing. He and the others went back to something they could understand. *"I'm going out to fish." (John 21:3)*

The call of Jesus is pretty simple.

"Follow me."

That's really all we have to do. The problem is, it's simple but not easy. Clear to understand, but confusing to do – at least some of the time.

OK, maybe a lot of the time

Jesus was the greatest leader and communicator of all time. He answered the great question we all have - *"what am I supposed to do with my life?"* – in simple and relatable terms.

"Follow Me, and I will make you fishers of men."
Matthew 4:19

Losing It All

In my life I've been blessed to achieve some of my dreams. And lose them too.

So back in the day, our music advertising business had been very successful for a good 15 year run. Then it started to decline and right around 911 (September 11, 2001) it took a nosedive. The business model and dynamics of our industry were changing rapidly, and our high overhead structure was not going to be sustainable.

We had to downsize. We put our house and the studio up for sale. Our small staff of six was gradually reduced to one, moi. Then, as the owner, eventually I laid off myself as president.

I'll never forget the morning I drove to state labor office and filed for unemployment. I sat in the lobby for about six hours waiting for the interview to apply for benefits. I had been the owner of a thriving business for ten years, now I needed that $200.00 dollar unemployment check just to make ends meet.

I left at the end of that day feeling completely humiliated.

Broken

As I was driving home, tears in my eyes, I felt the Holy Spirit say – "If you follow me, I will make you a fisher of men."

Over and over again I heard the call of God.

> *"If you follow me, I will make you a fisher of men."*

From the death of one dream, there was going to be the resurrection of another.

A better one, actually. I just didn't see it at the time.

Let Us Pray

"Lord today I pray for my brothers and sisters in the Lord, as well as myself. Give us a fresh vision, to move forward in your will and not backward. Thank you for the gift of redemption. Thank you for Your gift of re-creation. Help us to dream Your dream. To see with Your eyes. To fulfill our small part in Your story, for Your glory. In the name of the Father, Son and Holy Spirit. Amen."

11

Feed My Sheep

"If you love Me, feed My sheep." John 21:19 [Sunrise Photo April 11 2013]

Day 11 Feed My Sheep

> *Jesus said to him the third time, "Simon Peter, son of John, do you love Me" [with a deep, instinctive, personal affection for Me, as for a close friend]?*
>
> Peter was grieved (was saddened and hurt) that He should ask him the third time, 'Do you love Me?'
>
> And he said to Him, *"Lord, You know everything; You know that I love You"* [that I have a deep, instinctive, personal affection for You, as for a close friend].
>
> Jesus said to him, *"Feed My sheep."* John 21:19 Amplified Bible

Reinstatement

In my Bible, this conversation between Jesus and Peter is subtitled **"Jesus Reinstates Peter"**.

The definition of *reinstate* is to *"restore (someone or something) to their former position or condition."*

Peter had blown it in a big way. When the crisis came, he lost his head and his courage. He did what he swore he would never do. Deep grief and regret were wrapped around his psyche like huge prison chains.

He was never going to get over this.

Yet, despite his massive failure, Jesus still believed in Peter.

I have to apply this story to my own life. So do you.

This is good news.

Peter's story is not the only one. The Bible is the epic story of God re-storing, re-purposing, re-inventing, redeeming, *reinstating* – men and women who have betrayed and failed him.

My favorite example of course, is David, "the man after God's own heart". He is commended to all God followers as the example to follow (see Isaiah 55:4).

But there is also Abraham, Joseph, Moses, Gideon, Mary, Zacchaeus, Paul and many, many others.

Moving On

Notice that Jesus does not spend any energy breaking down what went wrong, the lessons to be learned, how to do better next time, etc. Monday morning quarterbacking was not relevant to Him.

Jesus checks Peter's heart. This is what matters.

If your heart is set in the right direction, God can use you.

This is the primary qualification for Jesus style, kingdom building leadership.

"Are you sure you love Me?"

Yes Lord.

"Then I have a very important mission for you and it's going to cost you your life. Take care of my sheep. Invest in them. Pour your life into them. Don't make the future about you, make it about them. I know I can trust you to do this."

On A Mission for God

The Jesus method of restoration is not just saying, "hey, we're cool, everything's ok, have a nice life."

Reinstatement means you can get back on course as a representative of Christ, to bring healing in this world.

The call of Jesus was not just for Peter, nor just for the leadership elite.

I believe every follower of Christ is called to be a leader in some context. You have sheep to shepherd, whether it's in the classroom, at the workplace, in your neighborhood, wherever.

Bloom where you are planted. *Lead.*

Jesus does not call us to be religious consumers. He calls each and every one of us to be fishers of men. To be leaders who care for his sheep.

You and I can do what Peter did. You can be a good shepherd.

The good shepherd knows "it's not about me." He lays down his life for his sheep.

> *I'll love Thee in life, I will love Thee in death,*
> *And praise Thee as long as Thou lendest me breath;*
> *And say when the death dew lies cold on my brow,*
> *If ever I loved Thee, my Jesus, 'tis now.*
> My Jesus I Love Thee 1864, Words: William R. Featherston, age 16

Let Us Pray:

"Jesus thank you for the gift of restoration. Help me to love You deeply, and from the overflow of that love – lead in a manner worthy of your trust. May Your kingdom come, and Your will be done, on earth as it is in heaven. In the name of the Father, Son and Holy Spirit. Amen."

12

A Servant Leader Movement

When I am weak, He is strong. 2 Corinthians 12:10 [Sunrise photo April 12, 2013]

Day 12 A Servant Leader Movement

Jesus said, *"Feed my sheep.*

*Very truly I tell you, when you were younger you dressed yourself and went where you wanted; but when you are old you will stretch out your hands, and someone else will dress you **and lead you where you do not want to go**."*

Jesus said this to indicate the kind of death by which Peter would glorify God.

Then he said to him, ***"Follow me!"*** John 21:18-19

Wherever He Leads I'll Go

During the 40 day period between his resurrection and ascension Jesus was preparing his disciples to change the world.

My guess is they didn't set out to do that.

"Hey guys let's change the world by doing what the master taught us and dying horrible deaths."

My guess is they were simply **doing the next right thing.**

They were so internally motivated by their personal encounter with Jesus, the incarnation of Truth and Love, that they were transformed.

> *"Jesus knew that he had to prepare his disciples for his ascension and return to the Father. He had to address the question of how he would continue to remain present with them and guide them in his physical absence. "* Robert E. Webber Ancient-Future Time page 154

My Heart is Steadfast

The resurrection changed everything. The Jesus tribe became very different people and *nothing,* no amount of pressure, would convince or coerce them to live any other way. These first followers of Jesus were absolutely resolved to completely follow His teaching and share the love of God with everyone.

They would do this by living a lifestyle that was radically different from the rest of the world. They marched to the beat of a different drummer. They lived from a value system that was *not of this world.*

Love Well

Selfless love was the identifying trait of His followers. They became the church by *radically* loving one another *and* loving outsiders. Jesus commissioned his followers to team up and co-labor together, literally to become His body – "the body of Christ" – as the continued presence of Jesus in the world.

The church itself is a sign of Jesus. So God's people must represent Jesus Christ and all that He taught.

Lead

Jesus taught the guiding model for leadership is the good shepherd.

A good shepherd is not on an ego trip. He does not misuse his power or authority. He is called to be a *servant leader.* Shepherds lead by example, relationship and serving first.

> *"The Son of Man came not to be served, but to serve and to give his life as a ransom for many."* Matthew 20:28

Do that and you change the world.

Let Us Pray

"Father help me to learn from the Good Shepherd, and help me to be a good shepherd. Lord you know my weaknesses and my failures, but when I am weak – You are strong. Empower me to bring You glory by serving well. May Your kingdom come, and Your will be done, on earth as it is in heaven. In the name of the Father, Son and Holy Spirit. Amen."

I Am Weak But You Are Strong!

> *I am weak, but Thou art strong;*
> *Jesus, keep me from all wrong;*
> *I'll be satisfied as long*
> *As I walk, let me walk close to Thee.*
> Just a Closer Walk With Thee (Traditional, Author Unknown)

13

Conspiracy Theory

8 So they [Martha and Mary] departed quickly from the tomb with fear and great joy, and ran to tell his disciples. 9 And behold, Jesus met them and said, "Greetings!" And they came up and took hold of his feet and worshipped him. 10 Then Jesus said to them, "Do not be afraid; go and tell my brothers to go to Galilee, and there they will see me." Matthew 28:8-10

Day 13 Conspiracy Theory

The Report of the Guard

> *11 While they were going, behold, some of the guard went into the city and told the chief priests all that had taken place. 12 And when they had assembled with the elders and taken counsel, they gave a sufficient sum of money to the soldiers 13 and said, "Tell people, 'His disciples came by night and stole him away while we were asleep.' 14 And if this comes to the governor's ears, we will satisfy him and keep you out of trouble." 15 So they took the money and did as they were directed. And this story has been spread among the Jews to this day.*
> Matthew 28:11-15

Terrified

For the soldiers on guard at the tomb, this should have been an easy assignment, *keep the dead man in his grave.* They were warriors in the world's most fearsome army, familiar with violence and war, and not afraid of … well, not much at all.

But they were terrified out of their minds when blinding light of the mighty angel streaked forth from heaven like lightning. With a thunderous roar the earth quaked as never before. And the grave opened up.

The guards were actually the first witnesses of the resurrection.

> *And behold, there was a great earthquake, for an angel of the Lord descended from heaven and came and rolled back the stone and sat on it. 3 His appearance was like lightning, and his clothing white as snow. 4 And for fear of him the guards trembled and became like dead men.* Matthew 28:2-4

Fear Not

The angel reassures Martha and Mary, *"Do not be afraid, for I know that you seek Jesus who was crucified. He is not here, for he has risen, as he said."*

Just seeing a real angel would turn my world upside down, but the news of His resurrection was electric – they ran excited, *"filled with fear and great joy."*

Lies, Lies, Lies

The complete opposite is the story of the soldiers and the religious establishment – the chef priests and elders.

How much lower could they go?

At every opportunity, the love of God incarnate was revealed to them, but they were blind to see it.

Driven to protect self-interest at all costs, murder of an innocent man consummated their madness.

The guards testified to the supernatural intervention at the tomb. This was unquestionably an act of God

Their response was to perpetuate a giant fraud. These were religious men, supposedly lovers of the Torah, now given over to Satanic deception. They bought off the guards, just like they bought off Judas. Sin begets more sin, and lies beget more lies.

This is the downward spiral of man at his worst. This is total depravity circa AD 33.

> *And this story has been spread among the Jews to this day.*

The Truth Will Set You Free

The truth came through because truth has enduring power. The effectiveness of fraud is very limited.

Eventually every thing comes to light.

Beginning with Martha and Mary, there was no stopping the truth.

The truth will set you free. *Jesus is alive!*

Let Us Pray

God, help me be a lover of truth. Keep my lips from willful deception. Create in me a pure heart, for the pure in heart will see God. Give me courage to stand for righteousness, even when it may be painful. In Jesus name, Amen.

14

Do This To Remember

Do this in remembrance of Me. Luke 22:19 [Sunrise photo April 14 2013]

[*The Resurrection of Christ*] Now, brothers and sisters, I want to remind you of the gospel I preached to you, which you received and on which you have taken your stand. For what I received I passed on to you as of first importance: that Christ died for our sins according to the Scriptures, that he was buried, that he was raised on the third day according to the Scriptures. 1 Corinthians 15:1, 3-4 NIV

Day 14 Do This To Remember

There is a fascinating insight from the Emmaus Road story in Luke 24. Cleopas and companion spent a day's journey walking and talking with Jesus. But they didn't realize who he was, until …

Until He broke bread with them.

> ^{30} *When he was at the table with them, he took bread, gave thanks, broke it and began to give it to them.* ^{31} *Then their eyes were opened and they recognized him.* Luke 24:30

We forget

On Resurrection Sunday (Easter), church goers around the world celebrate the most amazing, world changing , life altering event ever to happen in the history of the world.

For every follower of Christ, our personal history was changed as well.

Forever.

Yet for many people, Easter Sunday and its real life application can become a dull memory.

The only act of worship Jesus instituted

As far as I can tell, the only religious act of worship that Jesus commanded for His followers was The Lord's Supper (aka Holy Communion, the Eucharist).

¹⁹ And he took bread, gave thanks and broke it, and gave it to them, saying, "This is my body given for you; do this in remembrance of me." Luke 22:19

Robert Webber points out the pattern of worship outlined in this story.

> Liturgical scholarship finds in the Emmaus Road story the shape of early Christian worship.
>
> **We gather**
>
> **To hear Good News**
>
> **To break bread together**
>
> **To go forth and tell others**
>
> We knew Him in the breaking of the bread! (Robert E. Webber Ancient-Future Time page 154)

How to Do the Impossible

The mission of Jesus was to redeem the entire cosmos. He did this by atoning for the sins of the whole world. Then it was possible to empower ordinary men and women to do the extraordinary.

For the natural man, the mission of God is *Mission Impossible.*

But with God – the presence of God, the spirit of God, power of God indwelling us – all things are possible.

At the table – the breaking of bread and drinking from the cup – something profound happens. We remember Him. There is a fresh encounter with Jesus every time. His spirit fills and empowers us.

I have no idea how that actually happens. It just does.

At least it does for those who have faith.

Remember. Do.

Let Us Pray

"Jesus thank you for your life, your death and your resurrection. I am not worthy of your love and sacrifice. But I humble myself and accept your gift of grace. Help me to remember You, to honor You, to live and move and breathe for Your glory. May Your kingdom come, and Your will be done, on earth as it is in heaven. In the name of the Father, Son and Holy Spirit. Amen."

15

Truth or Lie?

We will speak the truth in love, growing in every way more and more like Christ Jesus. Ephesians 4:15 (NLT) [Sunrise Photo April 15, 2013]

Day 15 Truth or Lie ?

A True Testimony

> This is the disciple who testifies to these things and who wrote them down. **We know that his testimony is true.** John 21:24

> *33 They got up and returned at once to Jerusalem. There they found the Eleven and those with them, assembled together 34 and* **saying, "It is true! The Lord has risen** *and has appeared to Simon."* Luke 24:34

The quest for truth

I respect the doubt of the agnostic, or the skepticism of the atheist.

In my view, resistance to the Christian narrative, or really, any narrative of faith predicated on belief in the reality of the supernatural – could be the position of someone who is on a reasonable search for truth.

Of course this assumes the non-believer is actually reasonable and open to a world view that does not fit his paradigm.

Big assumption, but let's continue.

The quest for truth is a powerful driving force in the DNA of the human spirit. But there is always, at some level – a leap of faith required to actually believe, well, just about anything.

The witnesses in the gospel are speaking to anyone who would listen, really listen, to what they're saying – *"Look, we're not making this up. This is not a fairy tale. It is not a myth. We really saw this guy. It happened. It is true."*

And everyone who hears their message today has a choice to believe their testimony or not.

If it's not true, it's a big lie

> *If there's no resurrection, there's no living Christ. And face it—if there's no resurrection for Christ, everything we've told you is smoke and mirrors, and everything you've staked your life on is smoke and mirrors. Not only that, but we would be guilty of telling a string of barefaced lies about God, all these affidavits we passed on to you verifying that God raised up Christ—sheer fabrications, if there's no resurrection.* 1 Corinthians 15:13 (MSG)

Who cares about truth ?

Jesus cared about truth. In fact he claimed to be the Truth. Not only did He reveal truth, but He embodied truth.

> *^{37} Pilate said to Him, Then You are a King?*
>
> *Jesus answered, You say it! [You speak correctly!] For I am a King. [Certainly I am a King!]*
>
> *This is why I was born, and for this* **I have come into the world, to bear witness to the Truth**. *Everyone who is of the Truth [who is a friend of the Truth, who belongs to the Truth] hears and listens to My voice.* John 18:37 (AMP)
>
> *Everyone who cares for truth, who has any feeling for the truth, recognizes my voice.* MSG

This is written so that you may believe

If we really care about others, we will want to help them. We will "speak the truth in love" in order to bless and serve our fellow human beings. That was the motivation in John's writings as well as all the gospels.

> *But these are written that you may believe that Jesus is the Messiah, the Son of God, and that by believing you may have life in his name.* John 20:31

Ditto for moi. I hope these thoughts will help the reader to believe and truly have a super awesome life. 😀

Soli Deo Gloria!

Let Us Pray

From the Book of Common Prayer:

Almighty God, whom truly to know is everlasting life: Grant us so perfectly to know your Son Jesus Christ to be the way, the truth, and the life, that we may steadfastly follow his steps in the way that leads to eternal life; through Jesus Christ your Son our Lord, who lives and reigns with you, in the unity of the Holy Spirit, one God, forever and ever, Amen

16

Moses and the Prophets

A prayer for victims of violence. "Lord have mercy. Comfort the wounded, the grieving, and the despairing. May Your grace and peace surround and fill them. Touch those who are suffering with Your healing presence." [Sunrise photo April 16 2013]

Day 16 Moses and the Prophets

> *Then he started at the beginning, with the Books of Moses, and went on through all the Prophets, pointing out everything in the Scriptures that referred to him.* Luke 24:27

If I ever start a garage rock band I'm gonna name it : **Moses and The Prophets.** [Cue the drummer: *Ba-dum ching!*]

But seriously folks ....

Luke records four appearances of Jesus: to Peter, to the two disciples on the road to Emmaus, to the apostles as a group, and again to the apostles at his ascension. All of them took place in close proximity to Jerusalem.

The importance of Luke 24:27 is tremendous. Finally, the mystery of all this bible stuff is revealed.

I imagine one of the scriptures Jesus explains is Deuteronomy 6. This contains *The Shema,* the passage Jesus prescribes as the first and greatest commandment, sometimes paraphrased as *"Love God, love people".*

Remember God!

Deuteronomy 6 further commands God worshipers to be diligent to remember His ways and follow His principles for right living.

> *Write these commandments that I've given you today on your hearts. Get them inside of you and then get them inside your children. Talk about them wherever you are, sitting at home or walking in the street; talk about them from the time you get up in the morning to when you fall into bed at night. Tie them on your hands and foreheads as a reminder; inscribe them on the doorposts of your homes and on your city gates.* Deuteronomy 8:6-9 MSG

Connecting the dots

The Torah, the Psalms, the Prophets major and minor – finally it's all explained how it works together.

Jesus connects the dots.

From the beginning of the creation story there are clues given to God's plan for His rescue mission. The Jewish book of God's story is full of promises, predictions and foretelling of a coming savior. But you have to read between the lines to really get it.

Not anymore.

Plain talk.

Resurrection Jesus is done with parables and metaphorical illustrations. He is no longer a mere mortal speaking, He is the Son of God, *risen from the dead!*

Now his claims made perfectly good sense.

> *"Don't misunderstand why I have come. I did not come to abolish the law of Moses or the writings of the prophets. **No, I came to accomplish their purpose.**"* Matthew 5:17

Everything comes together through Jesus.

Word and Spirit work together

In the Emmaus Road story we see two truths come together.

First, the presence of Jesus **opens up the intellect** through the Word ("their eyes were opened").

Second, His Spirit **stirs the emotions** ("our hearts were burning").

The Word and the Spirit – the right hand and the left hand of God, come together. Jesus is magnified – made large - as both God *and* man.

It stirs my heart to sing: **Open the eyes of my heart Lord, I want to see You.** *(Paul Baloche)*

Let Us Pray

"Jesus open my mind to the truth of Your word. Stir my heart with passion for Your presence and Your ways. May your word and spirit come together in my life. Make me an instrument of Your peace. May Your kingdom come, and Your will be done, on earth as it is in heaven. In the name of the Father, Son and Holy Spirit. Amen."

How firm a foundation!

> *How firm a foundation, ye saints of the Lord,*
> *Is laid for your faith in His excellent Word!*
> *What more can He say than to you He hath said,*
> *You, who unto Jesus for refuge have fled?*
> Words: From A Selection of Hymns from the Best Authors, by John Rippon, 1787; attributed variously to John Keene, Kirkham, and John Keith.

17

What Is That To You?

"What is that to you? You must follow Me!" John 21:22 [Sunrise photo April 17, 2013]

Day 17 What is that to you?

²⁰ Peter turned and saw that the disciple whom Jesus loved was following them. (This was the one who had leaned back against Jesus at the supper and had said, "Lord, who is going to betray you?") ²¹ When Peter saw him, he asked, "Lord, what about him?"

²² Jesus answered, "If I want him to remain alive until I return, **what is that to you? You must follow me."**

²³ Because of this, the rumor spread among the believers that this disciple would not die. But Jesus did not say that he would not die; he only said, "If I want him to remain alive until I return, what is that to you?"

²⁴ This is the disciple who testifies to these things and who wrote them down. We know that his testimony is true. John 21:20-24

There's a lot of life application in this little exchange.

After all that time hanging around the Son of God, it appears that the master's teaching didn't rub off on the disciples.

Apparently they didn't understand Kingdom attitudes about **comparison, promotion** and **entitlement.**

What about him?

The disciples had favoritism issues with John. In Matthew 20, John's mom, Salome, makes a request that her sons – James and John, be promoted to a special position, at the right and left hand of Jesus in his kingdom. He replies, "lady you don't know what you're asking, and besides that, it's not my call"

Mom's idea did not sit well with John's colleagues. They took offense. They were *indignant.*

The disciples had gotten it all wrong. And so do you and I.

Wouldn't it be a wonderful thing if you were invited to a place of special honor? What if you got an invitation to a White House dinner?

I would like that. That would be pretty awesome.

Why should we *not* rejoice for someone "not me" being granted special privilege?

We can not earn the favor or grace of Almighty God, yet our Father's heart is generous. He delights in blessing His children. His ways are not our ways, and His gifts are to be appreciated.

Promotion comes from the Lord (Psalm 75:6). We should celebrate when our brothers or sisters are promoted. Even when it seems you are *overlooked.*

We deserve nothing. We're not entitled to *anything.* Resurrection people are empowered to **lose the entitlement mentality.**

> "*On your part, when you have done everything you were told to do, should say, 'We are unworthy servants; we have only done our duty.'*" Luke 17:10

But He gives us everything.

The greatest blessing comes from giving, from serving, from obeying. If we keep that mind set, we can receive his blessing. That is abundant living, when your life is about *more than you.*

After Jesus essentially tells Peter, "My deal with John is none of your business", his message seems to be:

"Your focus is being diverted. Don't be concerned about the assignments of your fellow laborers. Reorient your thinking. *Don't neglect the unique call I have given just for you.* Remember what you signed up for, to follow me – whatever the cost."

Jesus reminds us of his original call, simply – ***Follow Me!***

All To Jesus I Surrender

All to Jesus I surrender; all to him I freely give;
I will ever love and trust him, in his presence daily live.

Refrain:
I surrender all, I surrender all,
all to thee, my blessed Savior,
I surrender all.

All to Jesus I surrender; humbly at his feet I bow,
worldly pleasures all forsaken; take me, Jesus, take me now.

All to Jesus I surrender; make me, Savior, wholly thine;
fill me with thy love and power; truly know that thou art mine.

All to Jesus I surrender; Lord, I give myself to thee;
fill me with thy love and power; let thy blessing fall on me.

Let Us Pray

"Lord, all to Jesus I surrender. Help me to hear your voice today, answer your call, and follow wholeheartedly. Deliver me from comparison, self promotion, and feeling entitled to anything. I trust Your leadership in every aspect of my life. Your kingdom come. Your will be done. On earth as it is in heaven. In the name of the Father, Son and Holy Spirit. Amen."

18

Dressed in White

The one who overcomes will ... be dressed in white. Revelation 3:5 [Sunrise photo April 18 2013]

> *We will overcome by the blood of the Lamb and the word of our testimony.* Revelation 12:11

Day 18 Dressed in White

White is the liturgical color for the Easter season until the day of Pentecost. White is a traditional symbol of holiness, purity, worthiness. Here are some of my reflections on "white" for this season.

Angels are described as "dressed in white".

At the empty tomb

> *But Mary stood outside the tomb weeping. As she wept, she knelt to look into the tomb and saw two angels sitting there, **dressed in white**, one at the head, the other at the foot of where Jesus' body had been laid. They said to her, "Woman, why do you weep?"* John 20:10-12 (MSG)

On Ascension Hill

> *They were looking intently up into the sky as he was going, when suddenly two men **dressed in white** stood beside them.* Acts 1:9-11

White is the color of resurrection people, it marks Jesus people.

> *They will walk with me, **dressed in white**, for they are worthy.* ⁵ *The one who overcomes will, like them, be **dressed in white.*** Revelation 3:4-5

There's something about wearing white that just feels *clean.*

White signifies a season of hope and renewal

"White" and "spring" go together.

Spring is a beautiful season in middle Tennessee where I live. As I'm writing this and watching the sun rise, I hear hundreds of birds singing, a symphony of melodies and rhythms, themes and variation. The trees are now more green than grey. The breeze is gentle and pleasant. All nature is re-awakening. Life is in grow mode. And it seems inherently good.

Spring feels hopeful. But our hope is not in the cycle of nature, our hope is in *the risen one, who was dead but now is alive!*

That's something to sing about. Reminds me of one of my favorite hymns.

Fairest Lord Jesus

> *Fairest Lord Jesus, ruler of all nature,*
> *O thou of God and man the Son,*
> *Thee will I cherish, Thee will I honor,*
> *thou, my soul's glory, joy, and crown.*
>
> *Fair are the meadows, fairer still the woodlands,*
> *robed in the blooming garb of spring:*
> *Jesus is fairer, Jesus is purer*
> *who makes the woeful heart to sing.*
>
> *Fair is the sunshine, fairer still the moonlight,*
> *and all the twinkling starry host:*
> *Jesus shines brighter, Jesus shines purer*
> *than all the angels heaven can boast.*
>
> *Beautiful Savior! Lord of all the nations!*
> *Son of God and Son of Man!*
> *Glory and honor, praise, adoration,*
> *now and forevermore be thine.*

Suggestion: Wear something white for worship this season.

Let Us Pray

"Jesus you are Lord of all creation. All nature sings and the heavens declare Your glory. Thank you for Your gift of renewal, new life and new birth. Lord anoint me to be fruitful and multiply in this next season. For the glory of the Father, Son and Holy Spirit. Amen."

19

Peace Be With You

Peace of mind and heart is a gift the world can not give. So don't be troubled or afraid. John14:27 [Sunrise photo April 19 2013]

Day 19 Peace Be With You

While they were saying all this, Jesus appeared to them and said, "Peace be with you." They thought they were seeing a ghost and were scared half to death. Luke 24:36-37.

Luke 24: 36-49 describes one of the twelve Jesus resurrection appearances. This passage is rich with insights. Take a moment to read it when you have a chance. We'll focus on just one aspect today and more next time.

Disoriented

Imagine the scene that Sunday evening. Consider the disciples' state of mind. All eleven of Jesus closest friends were gathered together, trying to figure out what was going on.

Their leader had been an exceptional human being, a man unlike any they had ever encountered. His example, his embodiment of love, his holy presence, his miraculous power - had completely and thoroughly wrecked their lives.

His brutal and bloody execution was still vivid in their consciousness. *How was it possible?*

It was inconceivable that Jesus could possibly be alive. He had done what? Come back from the dead? *How was that possible?* They couldn't believe it.

They were utterly disoriented. They had to process this together. Confusion and disbelief were mixed with hopeful expectation. But there was no clarity about what was happening.

Then Jesus interrupts their meeting in the middle of the conversation.

Party crasher

All of a sudden, out of nowhere, Jesus – the ultimate party crasher, just appears from behind locked doors.

Maybe it looked like a scene from the old Star Trek show, like he was being transported from the Starship Enterprise. *"Scotty, beam me down. Energize."*

His appearance had the element of surprise which "startled and frightened them."

Surprise!

I don't know abut you, but when I am startled, my heart skips a beat, I gasp and do a little leap in the air. All in an instant.

This scene has played out more than a few times in our kitchen.

I'll be deep in concentration making my morning coffee, and thinking about, well, worship dude stuff. Our daughter Faith will innocently ~~sneak~~ walk into the room, but I don't see her.

My mind is somewhere else (this is my usual state of mind, just ask my wife). When I turn around and suddenly see Faith there, I jump out of my skin – "startled" and maybe a little bit frightened. *"Sheesh, you scared me!"*

Does something like this ever happen to you?

I didn't think so. Back to our devotional …

It's gonna be OK

The disciples were understandably freaking out. This is the first thing Jesus addresses.

> *Shalom Alechem (שלום עליכם)*

"Peace be with you". It was a traditional greeting of their culture, but now it has *a new meaning.*

The Prince of Peace was there to give them the gift of peace. Yes, peace for that moment, but even more so, eternally in every aspect of their lives.

> *"You had me at hello"* – Dorothy to Jerry in the movie
> "Jerry McGuire"

Jesus knew the chaos and turmoil that was to come for them, and also for you and for me. The first blessing of his resurrected presence is proof of "Peace".

Right now, in every circumstance, Jesus offers us lasting peace that is beyond understanding.

> *"I am leaving you with a gift–peace of mind and heart. And the peace I give is a gift the world cannot give. So don't be troubled or afraid."* John 14:27

The peace of God is a free gift. Receive it. May the Lord be with you today!

Let Us Pray

From the Book of Common Prayer:

Almighty God, kindle, we pray, in every heart the true love of peace, and guide with your wisdom those who take counsel for the nations of the earth, that in tranquility your dominion may increase until the earth is filled with the knowledge of your love; through Jesus Christ our Lord, who lives and reigns with you, in the unity of the Holy Spirit, one God, now and for ever. Amen.

20

Ghost Busters

"Don't be afraid. Take courage. I am with you" Matthew 14:27 [Sunrise photo April 20 2013]

Day 20 Ghost Busters

*^{37} They were startled and frightened, **thinking they saw a ghost.** ^{38} He said to them, "Why are you troubled, and why do doubts rise in your minds? ^{39} Look at my hands and my feet. It is I myself! Touch me and see; **a ghost does not have flesh and bones, as you see I have."***

^{40} When he had said this, he showed them his hands and feet. ^{41} And while they still did not believe it because of joy and amazement, he asked them, "Do you have anything here to eat?" ^{42} They gave him a piece of broiled fish, ^{43} and he took it and ate it in their presence. Luke 24:37-43

As best I can tell, a biblical Christian worldview does not adhere to the existence of "ghosts", defined as "a disembodied spirit imagined, usually as a vague, shadowy or evanescent form, as wandering among or haunting living persons."

But the beliefs and worldview of the ancient world were quite different from our modern scientific era. The possibility that ghosts were 'out there' was very real in the minds of the disciples.

This wasn't the first time they confused Jesus with being a ghost.

Remember the account of Jesus walking on water ? (See Matthew 14, Mark 6, John 6)

*At about four o'clock in the morning, Jesus came toward them walking on the water. They were scared out of their wits. **"A ghost!"** they said, crying out in terror.*

^{27} But Jesus was quick to comfort them. "Courage, it's me. Don't be afraid."

Jesus makes it very clear in both accounts – "No, I'm not a ghost".

He also makes it clear , when you're scared out of your mind, turn to Jesus.

"Take courage, I am here."

The message Jesus gives is two fold.

First, be at peace, don't stay afraid, don't remain full of fear.

Then, take heart, be filled with courage. Take action. **I am here to help you.**

So, may boldness arise in you today!

Stand Up Stand Up For Jesus

> *Stand up, stand up for Jesus, ye soldiers of the cross;*
> *Lift high His royal banner, it must not suffer loss.*
> *From victory unto victory His army shall He lead,*
> *Till every foe is vanquished, and Christ is Lord indeed.*
> Words: George Duffield, Jr., 1858.

Let Us Pray

From the Book of Common Prayer:

For Quiet Confidence
O God of peace, you have taught us that in returning and rest we shall be saved, in quietness and confidence shall be our strength: By the might of your Spirit lift us, we pray, into your presence, where we may be still and know that you are God; through Jesus Christ our Lord. Amen.

21

Wait Until

O Master let me walk with thee. [Sunrise photo April 21 2013]

Day 21 Until you're equipped with power from on high

> *He went on to open their understanding of the Word of God, showing them how to read their Bibles this way.*
>
> *He said, "You can see now how it is written that the Messiah suffers, rises from the dead on the third day, and then a total life-change through the forgiveness of sins is proclaimed in his name to all nations—starting from here, from Jerusalem!*
>
> *You're the first to hear and see it. You're the witnesses.*
>
> *What comes next is very important: I am sending what my Father promised to you, so stay here in the city until he arrives,* **until you're equipped with power from on high.***"* Luke 24:45-49 MSG

Today marks the 21st day and the third Sunday after Resurrection Sunday. We're almost halfway there. Time ticks on...

This is another passage deep in meaning and significance.

Jesus is teaching, advising and directing his followers. He's helping them figure out what is happening. He concludes by instructing them *stay here and wait until you're empowered ....*

I'm not a big fan of waiting.

There's a life lesson here about the divine timing of God.

God has an organization – a wise sequencing of circumstances. His ways baffles my logic most of the time.

Does that seem true to you, too?

God takes the things that seem long delayed, random, happenstance and outright wrong – then He uses them for *good.*

I think Jesus is saying here, *"Wait and trust the timing of God. It's gonna be amazing."*

When we get out of God's timing, things break down. Let's walk in step with the Master.

O Master Let Me Walk With Thee

O Master, let me walk with Thee,
In lowly paths of service free;
Tell me Thy secret; help me bear
The strain of toil, the fret of care.

Help me the slow of heart to move
By some clear, winning word of love;
Teach me the wayward feet to stay,
And guide them in the homeward way.

Teach me Thy patience; still with Thee
In closer, dearer, company,
In work that keeps faith sweet and strong,
In trust that triumphs over wrong.

In hope that sends a shining ray
Far down the future's broadening way,
In peace that only Thou canst give,
With Thee, O Master, let me live.

Words: Washington Gladden, 1879

Let Us Pray

"Jesus thank you that your words are the words of life. Fill us with the fruit of your Holy Spirit today. Love, joy, peace, patience, kindness, goodness, gentleness and self control. Help me to walk in your ways, and trust the process of my heavenly Father. May Your kingdom come, and Your will be done, on earth as it is in heaven. In the name of the Father, Son and Holy Spirit. Amen."

22

The Power of An Opened Mind

Be transformed by the renewing of your mind. Romans 12:2 [Sunrise photo April 22]

Day 22 He Opened Their Minds

Then he said, "Everything I told you while I was with you comes to this: All the things written about me in the Law of Moses, in the Prophets, and in the Psalms have to be fulfilled." (Luke 24:44 MSG)

Then He [thoroughly] opened up their minds to understand the Scriptures. (Luke 24:45 AMP)

According to the *Encyclopedia of Biblical Prophecy* there are a total of 1,817 Biblical prophecies; 1,239 are in the Old Testament, and 578 are in the New Testament. These 1,817 prophecies involve 8,352 of the Bible's verses. Since there are 31,124 verses altogether in the Bible, the number of *prophetic* verses amounts to about 27 percent, or *one-fourth* of the total number of verses in the Bible.

Scholars report over 300 Messianic prophecies about Jesus. These include several dozen major, direct prophecies along with scores and scores of Messianic scriptures that include allusions, hints, types, foreshadowings, and Messianic clues in the Old Testament.

That's a lot of data.

Information overload.

I say this a lot – *"The Bible is a big book with a lot of information."*

Luke records *"He [thoroughly] opened up their minds to understand the Scriptures".* My mind can not comprehend what this fully means.

The way Jesus opens the mind to understand is **beyond cognitive reasoning.** It is not taught by lecture or explanation. It is beyond learning.

It is imparted. It is received by and through experiencing the presence and spirit of Jesus. This is a transcendent exchange.

Scholarship and "book learning" alone will not transform your life.

What brings about life change that impacts the world? A mind "opened up" by the Spirit of God to truly understand the Word of God.

Paul says this in Romans 12:2

> *... Be transformed (changed) by the [entire] renewal of your mind [by its new ideals and its new attitude] ...*

Let Us Pray

"Lord I pray for a renewed mind. Open my mind as you did for your disciples, to understand the wonders in Your word. You are good, and your love endures forever! May Your kingdom come, and Your will be done, on earth as it is in heaven. In the name of the Father, Son and Holy Spirit. Amen."

23

Proclaim Repentance and Forgiveness

Repentance and forgiveness will totally change your life. Tell somebody the good news. Luke24:47 [Sunrise photo April 23 2013]

Day 23 Proclaim Repentance and Forgiveness of Sins

⁴⁵ Then he opened their minds to understand the Scriptures, ⁴⁶ and said to them, "Thus it is written, that the Christ should suffer and on the third day rise from the dead, ⁴⁷ and that repentance and forgiveness of sins should be proclaimed in his name to all nations, beginning from Jerusalem. ⁴⁸ You are witnesses of these things. Luke 24:45-48

Jesus explained to the disciples, from the scriptures, why he had to suffer and die as the fulfillment of God's promise. He showed how all humanity could now be brought into right relationship with the Holy One.

His resurrection was irrefutable proof. He knew what He was talking about. He was the ultimate authority.

In the same sentence Jesus commissioned his followers to proclaim *repentance and forgiveness of sins to all nations.*

Love follows through.

Love makes and keeps a promise. Love takes action.

This is The Message Peter and the other apostles boldly declared in the Temple courts in Acts 5:29-32.

²⁹ Peter and the other apostles replied: "We must obey God rather than human beings! ³⁰ The God of our ancestors raised Jesus from the dead—whom you killed by hanging him on a cross. ³¹ God exalted him to his own right hand as Prince and Savior that he might bring Israel to repentance and forgive their sins. ³² We are witnesses of these things, and so is the Holy Spirit, whom God has given to those who obey him." Acts 5:29-45

They were unstoppable.

This story – *the good news that will change your life* – is what all followers of Jesus are to perpetuate, to pass on, and to share.

Matthew Henry's Commentary of Luke 24:47

Written hundreds of years ago, Matthew Henry (1662-1714) continues to inspire today.

> [2.] The great gospel duty of repentance must be pressed upon the children of men. Repentance for sin must be preached in Christ's name, and by his authority, Luke 24:47. All men every where must be called and commanded to repent, Acts 17:30. "Go, and tell all people that the God that made them, and the Lord that bought them, expects and requires that, immediately upon this notice given, they turn from the worship of the gods that they have made to the worship of the God that made them; and not only so, but from serving the interests of the world and the flesh; they must turn to the service of God in Christ, must mortify all sinful habits, and forsake all sinful practices. Their hearts and lives must be changed, and they must be universally renewed and reformed."

Henry points out that men make idols of the things of this world and the flesh.

The heart energy of pursuing these desires is an expression of *worship*.

Repentance sets worship in the right direction

Repentance is turning the direction of our worship away from *"all those vain things that charm me most"* (Watts) towards the One most worthy of our heart's affections.

Without repentance, worship is headed in the wrong direction. Repentance is course correction.

Let Us Pray

"Jesus thank you for your life, death and resurrection. I repent from my idol worship, of serving a worldly agenda and my fleshly desires. I turn my heart fully to You – to honor, adore, obey and worship You alone. Thank you for forgiving my sins. Help me to boldly proclaim this good news everywhere you place me. May Your kingdom come, and Your will be done, on earth as it is in heaven. In the name of the Father, Son and Holy Spirit. Amen."

24

To All Nations

Let your light shine! Matthew 5:16 [Sunrise photo April 24 2013]

Day 24 Preach this among all nations

> *⁴⁷ It was also written that this message would be proclaimed in the authority of his name **to all the nations**, beginning in Jerusalem: 'There is forgiveness of sins for all who repent.'* Luke 24:47

Jesus gave his followers their mission in S.M.A.R.T. goal format.

It was *Specific, Measurable, Attainable, Relevant and Timely.* This mission would require many generations of commitment, and is still on-going.

Specific - *proclaim the message of forgiveness of sins for all who repent*

Measurable – *to all nations*

Attainable – *start with Jerusalem (start where you are, with those closest to you)*

Relevant – *offer to solve the problem of sin, this is always relevant*

Time-bound - *begin now and keep at it until the return of Christ*

As the *internet generation,* we live in the most exciting period in history.

It has never been more feasible to reach every nation – every ethnicity, every people group on the face of the earth – than it is right now, in our generation.

You can hop on a plane and affordably be on the other side of the world in a day, two at the most. It is an amazing era.

I've had the wonderful opportunity to do that every summer for the last 12 years. I can lead worship in Nashville on Sunday morning, board a plane Sunday afternoon, and be sharing the gospel in Romania on Monday afternoon.

I know – it's modern technology. But it feels like a miracle to me.

This was unthinkable just 100 years ago. **Today, every nation is reachable.** Pray for missionaries near and far, long term and short term, men and women willing to go and share the gospel.

Let Us Pray

"Jesus thank you for the gift of Your forgiveness for all who repent. We call forth the nations, that every knee will bow and every tongue confess that Jesus Christ is King of Kings and Lord of Lords. We pray for harvesters. May Your light shine in us and through us, and bring glory to our heavenly Father. In Jesus name, Amen."

25

Why Jerusalem?

For I am not ashamed of the gospel of Christ: for it is the power of God unto salvation to every one that believes; to the Jew first, and also to the Gentile. Romans 1:16 [Sunrise photo April 25 2013]

Day 25 Start With Jerusalem

*Scripture also says that by the authority of Jesus people would be told to turn to God and change the way they think and act so that their sins will be forgiven. This would be told to people from all nations, **beginning in the city of Jerusalem.*** Luke 24:47 GOD'S WORD® Translation (©1995)

Why Jerusalem? Why did Jesus say begin here?

John 3:16 says *"For God so loved the world that he gave ... "* everything.

God, out of his mercy, initiated the redemption of all creation by making and keeping a promise to the Jewish people, the seed of Abraham.

The gospel *"is the power of God unto salvation to every one that believes; **to the Jew first,** and also to the Gentile."* Romans 1:16

God did not react to the rejection of the Jews by rejecting them in turn – no, he made the way for reconciliation.

"... beginning in Jerusalem"

Jerusalem was the scene of the story, this is where it all happened.

> "The Saviour's disciples were to begin where the prophets had prophesied, and had been put to death; where sinners had rejected God's voice times out of mind." CH Spurgeon Sermon "Beginning at Jerusalem"

Why Jerusalem? 8 Reasons

(Quotes from the CH Spurgeon Sermon "Beginning at Jerusalem")

1. In fulfillment of the Scripture prophecies.

See Isaiah 2:3, Joel 2:37, Obadiah v.27, Zechariah 14:8

"Because the Bible said so, therefore they must begin at Jerusalem, and I call your attention to this, for our Lord Jesus was particular that every jot and tittle of the Old Testament should be fulfilled."

2. The gospel story began in Jerusalem.

"It was at Jerusalem that the facts which make up the gospel had occurred. It was there that Jesus Christ died, that he was buried, that he rose again, and that he ascended into heaven."

3. God's love for the Jewish people

"The third reason why the Lord Jesus told them to begin at Jerusalem may have been that *he knew that there would come a time when some of his disciples would despise the Jews,* and therefore he said—When you preach my gospel, begin with them. This is a standing commandment, and everywhere we ought to preach the gospel to the Jew as well as to the Gentile; Paul even says, 'to the Jew first.'"

4. Begin where you are tempted not to begin.

"The fourth reason for beginning at Jerusalem is a practical lesson for you. We ought always to try to do good where we think that it will not succeed. If we have a very strong aversion as a token that we are not called to it, we may regard it as a sign that we ought at least to try it."

5. Begin at home.

"Beginning at Jerusalem,' must surely mean *begin at home."*

Family, co-workers, neighbors – share the gospel by the way you live and speak with those close to you. Make it your first priority to bear witness to those with whom you regularly live and interact.

6. It was a tough audience.

Jerusalem was a religious center. They had been there, done that. Their hearts were hard.

"Wherefore, in working for Christ, do not hesitate to go to those who have refused the gospel hitherto, for you may yet prevail."

7. The time was short.

Jerusalem was to be destroyed by the Romans just 70 years later. Life is short. Spurgeon says to be bold, especially with those who are old, sick or you may never see again.

"When you meet with a pining case, do not wait to be introduced, but introduce yourself; and tenderly, gently, quietly, lovingly say a word about coming to Christ at once. We ought speedily to look up those whose day of grace is short."

8. Opposition is to be engaged with, not retreated from.

"Begin courageously where you may expect opposition."

The greatest sinners are the objects of the greatest mercy.

Let Us Pray

I invite you to pray with me today.

"Jesus I want to live in agreement with Your word, that I would be 'not ashamed of the gospel of Jesus Christ, for it is the power of God unto salvation, first to the Jew, and then to everyone else'. Lord I pray for the peace of Jerusalem. May Your kingdom come, and Your will be done, on earth as it is in heaven. In the name of the Father, Son and Holy Spirit. Amen."

26

The Power of Witness

Your love O Lord reaches to the heavens, your faithfulness to the skies. Psalm 36:5 [Sunrise photo April 26 2013]

Day 26 The Power of Witness

> *You're the first to hear and see it. You're the witnesses.* Luke 24:48

A witness, according to Webster's dictionary, is *"one that gives evidence; specifically : one who testifies in a cause or before a judicial tribunal; one who has personal knowledge of something".*

I'm not a lawyer, but I've watched quite a few lawyer shows – so of course, I'm an expert.

All the drama is in what the witness has to say.

The eyewitness account is the hinge of the drama. He or she is the most valuable, credible source, because they were there. They take an oath "to tell the whole truth so help me God" to simply report the facts of what they saw and experienced.

Now in this passage from Luke, Jesus is saying, *"here's how you do it"* – just tell others your story, what you saw, heard and experienced.

These original eyewitnesses had an unbelievable story, but nothing could deter them from just telling the truth. Their story is what literally changed the world.

Deep and Wide

Andy Stanley describes how the power of witness birthed the church in his book Deep & Wide: Creating Churches Unchurched People Love to Attend:

> *In the beginning, the church was a gloriously messy movement with a laser-focused message and a global mission.*
>
> *It was led by men and women who were fueled not by what they believed, but by what they had seen.*

That simple fact sets the church apart from every other religious movement in the history of the world.

After all, it wasn't the teaching of Jesus that sent his followers to the streets. It was his resurrection.

The men and women who made up the nucleus of the church weren't simply believers in an abstract philosophy or even faithful followers of a great leader; they were eyewitnesses of an event.

Andy Stanley, **Deep & Wide** (Kindle location 505)

Evangelism

Evangelism is simply telling the story of God at work in your life.

If you don't have much of a story, you might want to work on that.

Start by taking a risk. Do *something for God* outside of your comfort zone. Do it for Jesus sake.

And tell the story!

I Love To Tell The Story

> I love to tell the story of unseen things above,
> of Jesus and his glory, of Jesus and his love.
> I love to tell the story, because I know 'tis true;
> it satisfies my longings as nothing else can do.
> Refrain:
> I love to tell the story, 'twill be my theme in glory,
> to tell the old, old story of Jesus and his love.
>
> *Text: Katherine Hankey, 1834-1911*

Let Us Pray

"Lord thank you for your grace, your kindness, Your Presence! Your mercies are new every morning. Help me today, bear witness of Your goodness to everyone I encounter. Take me out of my comfort zone and into the make-a-difference zone. Give me grace to share Your great love humbly, honestly, compassionately, and winsomely – for Your glory. In the name of the Father, Son and Holy Spirit. Amen."

27

What Are You Waiting For?

Those who hope in The Lord shall renew their strength; they shall run and not grow weary Isaiah 40:31 [A rainy sunrise photo April 27 2013]

Day 27 What Are You Waiting For?

> *"What comes next is very important: I am sending what my Father promised to you, so stay here in the city until he arrives, until you're equipped with power from on high."* Luke 24:49

In this resurrection appearance, Jesus has encouraged the disciples and given them an audacious mission. Then he tells them their next step is *not* to "get out there and go for it".

No, they are to wait.

Timing is important. Maybe timing is everything. Doing the right thing at the wrong time never works.

The reason for waiting on the Lord is powerful – to be empowered by God. You gotta do God's work , God's way. You can not do the work of the ministry on your own strength.

I'm not so sure *why* waiting is one of God's methods. God's ways are not our ways. He will give us many opportunities to learn this and trust him more deeply.

Be encouraged, God is in the waiting.

> *But those who wait on the Lord*
> *Shall renew their strength;*
> *They shall mount up with wings like eagles,*
> *They shall run and not be weary,*
> *They shall walk and not faint.*
> Isaiah 40:31

In his commentary on Luke 24:49 John Gill (1697 – 1771) an English Baptist pastor, biblical scholar, and theologian understood the disciples were to *wait on the Lord* in prayer and silence:

> *But tarry ye in the city of Jerusalem; for the space of ten days; here they were to continue during that time, and not depart*

> *thence; yea, they were to sit there, as the word used signifies: they were to sit still, and be silent; they were not to begin to preach; they were only to attend to prayer and Christian conversation, and to wait for the Spirit, the promise of the Father; and who also is designed in the following clause: until ye be endued with power from on high ...*

Obedience is a test of character. God is continually developing our character.

In times of waiting, the fruit of the Holy Spirit is sown deeper in our character. With the right attitude, we can increase in love, joy, peace, patience, kindness, goodness, faithfulness, gentleness and self-control. (Galatians 5:22)

Jesus made a promise *"I am sending to you what my Father promised."* When he delivered, it was amazing.

What God can and will do with those willing to wait upon Him is still amazing.

Let Us Pray

"Lord thank you for the gift of your Spirit. I ask for more of the fruit of Your Spirit to grow in my character. My hope is in You. Give me patience to wait upon You. May your kingdom come, and Your will be done. On earth as it is in heaven. In the name of the Father, Son and Holy Spirit. Amen."

28

We Gather Together

*And they spent all of their time in the Temple, praising God. Luke 24:53
[Sunrise photo from January 5 2013, today April 28, was a cloudy day.]*

Day 28 We Gather Together

> *⁵³ And they stayed continually at the temple, praising God.*
>
> *⁵³ And they were continually in the temple celebrating with praises and blessing and extolling God. Amen (so be it).* Luke 24:53 *(NIV , AMP)*

Today marks the the 4th Sunday of Easter. Believers in the resurrection will gather in places of worship all over the globe, as they have for over two thousand years. They will do this in remembrance of Him.

We will tell the story, God's story. Followers will share testimonies of God's grace in their lives.

> *Everywhere they went, followers of The Way insisted that God had done something unique in their generation; he had raised a man from the dead.* Andy Stanley

The fact that the church exists is one of the greatest witnesses of the power of Jesus resurrection.

> *But the story of the church is not just unexplainable, it's undeniable. Today over a third of the world's population claims some kind of faith in Jesus. The Roman Empire is long gone. Ancient Judaism died with the destruction of the Jewish temple in AD 70. But today one third of the world's population claims Jesus as the centerpiece of their religious experience. He taught for three years, and twenty centuries later, he is worshiped on every continent on the planet. That's an amazing story. It's a story every Christian and church attendee should know. And as church leaders, it's a story in which we have the privilege of participating. Actually, it's a story we are responsible for shaping. Like it or not, we are the stewards of the church for our generation. More daunting than that is the fact that we determine what comes to mind for the next generation when they hear the term church.* Stanley, Andy (2012-09-25). Deep & Wide:

Creating Churches Unchurched People Love to Attend (Kindle Locations 532-539). Zondervan. Kindle Edition.

In our generation, let us rediscover the heart of God as we live and move and breathe as his people, the church.

The Lord be with you this Lord's day!

Let Us Pray

"Lord today we pray for your church. We ask for unity, for the knowledge of Your will, for your Holy Spirit to move, and for fruitfulness. Bless your leaders, bless their congregations. May your kingdom come, and Your will be done. On earth as it is in heaven. In the name of the Father, Son and Holy Spirit. Amen."

29

What Did He Promise?

All of God's promises have been fulfilled in Christ. Yes and Amen! 2 Corinthians 1:20 [Sunrise photo April 29 2013}

Day 29 What Did He Promise?

> *I am going to send you **what my Father has promised;** but stay in the city until you have been clothed with power from on high."* Luke 24:49

Jesus is referring to the coming power of the Spirit prophesied in Joel 2:28-29 and fulfilled in Acts 2:4 (NIV concordance).

"The promise was that they should be aided by the power of the Holy Spirit" (Barnes commentary)

Note these three promises Jesus made about the gift of the Holy Spirit:

1. You'll know what to say to proclaim the gospel. The Holy Spirit will communicate through you.

> *"... don't worry about what to say or how to say it. When the time comes, you will be given what to say."* Matthew 10:19

2. The Spirit of truth will live in you and be in you.

> *And I will ask the Father, and he will give you another advocate to help you and be with you forever— the Spirit of truth. The world cannot accept him, because it neither sees him nor knows him. But you know him, for he lives with you and will be in you.* John 14:16-17

3. The Spirit will teach you and reveal to you the things of Jesus.

> *But the Advocate, the Holy Spirit, whom the Father will send in my name, will teach you all things and will remind you of everything I have said to you.* John 14:26

The presence of the Holy Spirit in a man or woman of God does the talking for them. If you commit to being the right kind of person, God does the heavy lifting.

This is a truth and a promise we can rely on, and is especially relevant when we lead worship.

Standing on The Promises

*Standing on the promises I cannot fall,
listening every moment to the Spirit's call,
resting in my Savior as my all in all,
standing on the promises of God.*
Text & Music R. Kelso Carter, 1849-1926

Let Us Pray

I invite you to pray with me today.

"Father thank you that your promises are Yes and Amen through Jesus Christ our Lord. Thank you for the gift of your Spirit, may it speak in, through and to me today. Your kingdom come, and Your will be done on earth as it is in heaven. In Jesus name. Amen."

30

Power From On High

In Him was Life, and the Life was the Light of men. John1:4 [Sunrise April 30 2013]

Hurray! We're 30 days into the series! I'm loving this project, hope it's a blessing to you too!

Day 30 Power From On High

> *"And behold, I will send forth upon you what My Father has promised; but remain in the city [Jerusalem] **until you are clothed with power from on high.**"* Luke 24:49 (AMP)

> *"And now I will send the Holy Spirit, just as my Father promised. But stay here in the city **until the Holy Spirit comes and fills you with power from heaven.**"* Luke 24:49 (MSG)

Power from heaven is ALL POWERFUL!

Power from on high originates in *El Elyon,* the Most High God.

It is an attribute of *El Shaddai,* God Almighty.

When the power of heaven touches earth, it produces not only amazing signs, wonders and miracles – but a *sense of awe* worthy of *El Hannora,* the Awesome God.

> *Endued with power from on high – The power which would be given them by the descent of the Holy Spirit – the power of speaking with tongues, of working miracles, and of preaching the gospel with the attending blessing and aid of the Holy Spirit. This was accomplished in the gift of the Holy Spirit on the day of Pentecost.* (Barnes commentary)

Jesus promised in John 14:12 that his followers would be able to do *what only God could do* when they were empowered by his Holy Spirit.

> *"I can guarantee this truth: Those who believe in me will do the things that I am doing. **They will do even greater things because I am going to the Father."*** GOD'S WORD® Translation (©1995)

Jesus prophesied that after his resurrection and ascension, we would do even greater things than He did! Did you get that? *Greater things!* This promise is for Jesus followers now, in every generation.

That idea blows my mind because it seems so *preposterous.*

But it's right there in black and white – or red, depending on your Bible. You gotta do something with that verse. Either ignore it or act on it.

I choose to believe it.

Let Us Pray

> O God the Holy Ghost
> Who art light unto thine elect
> Evermore enlighten us.
> Thou who art fire of love
> Evermore enkindle us.
> Thou who art Lord and Giver of Life,
> Evermore live in us.
> Thou who bestowest sevenfold grace,
> Evermore replenish us.
> As the wind is thy symbol,
> So forward our goings.
> As the dove, so launch us heavenwards.
> As water, so purify our spirits.
> As a cloud, so abate our temptations.
> As dew, so revive our languor.
> As fire, so purge our dross
> *Christina Rossetti (AD 1830-1894)*
>
> Amen.

31

Just As He Told You

Light of the world you stepped down into darkness, opened my eyes, made me see. Here I am to worship! (c) Tim Hughes/worshiptogether.com [Sunrise May 1 2013]

Day 31 Just as He Told You

> *⁶ But the angel said, "Don't be alarmed. You are looking for Jesus of Nazareth, who was crucified. He isn't here! He is risen from the dead! Look, this is where they laid his body. ⁷ Now go and tell his disciples, including Peter, that Jesus is going ahead of you to Galilee. You will see him there, **just as he told you before he died.**"* Mark 16:6-7 (NLT)

Jesus was physically present for forty days after his resurrection, sharing life with his friends and followers. During that time, I'm sure they were processing all they had learned from him before he died.

This was the paradigm shift of all paradigm shifts. Now all of his words, all of his teaching had a new perspective – one of absolute authority.

Jesus was not only absolutely right, he was absolutely trustworthy. His word was better than money in the bank.

"Just as he told you before he died…"

His manifesto was the Sermon on the Mount (Matthew 5-7). Jesus lived a life and taught principles that were contrary to human nature – love your enemies, turn the other cheek, give with no strings attached, be pious in private, ask God boldly for what you want, choose the narrow road; evaluate by results, not just good intentions.

Jesus was not teaching just "good ideas" you could take or leave. Jesus was teaching absolute truth that would change your life for the better. No doubt about it.

The proof is in the resurrection.

The Resurrection is more than a onetime event to be commemorated or even celebrated. It is a lifetime call to completely trust and follow the Son of God.

Let Us Pray

"Lord help us remember the truth you have taught in your word. Help us to trust you completely. Thank you for the power of your resurrection living in us right now. May we give you glory in all that we say and do. In Jesus name, Amen."

Trust and Obey

>When we walk with the Lord
>in the light of his word,
>what a glory he sheds on our way!
>While we do his good will,
>he abides with us still,
>and with all who will trust and obey.
>Trust and obey,
>for there's no other way
>to be happy in Jesus,
>but to trust and obey.
>***Text:*** *John H. Sammis, 1846-1919*

32

500 Witnesses

He revealed his glory, and his disciples believed in him. John 2:11 [Sunrise pic by Rob Still, May 2 2013]

Day 32 Five Hundred Witnesses

> *3 For what I received I passed on to you as of first importance: that Christ died for our sins according to the Scriptures, 4 that he was buried, that he was raised on the third day according to the Scriptures, 5 and that he appeared to Cephas, and then to the Twelve. 6 After that, he appeared to more than five hundred of the brothers and sisters at the same time, most of whom are still living, though some have fallen asleep. 7 Then he appeared to James, then to all the apostles, 8 and last of all he appeared to me also, as to one abnormally born.*
> 1 Corinthians 15:3-8

In this passage, Paul reports what must have been common knowledge among the followers of the Way. Five hundred folks had seen the risen Jesus. Many were still alive when he wrote this and could verify the facts.

This documents that Jesus was seen by hundreds of people, many more than just the eleven disciples. Some traditions hold this was on Mt. Tabor in Galilee.

"One thing is proved by this, that the Lord Jesus had many more disciples than is generally supposed." [Barnes commentary]

Paul traces his personal spiritual connection to the resurrection.

> *8 Last of all, as though I had been born at the wrong time, I also saw him. 9 For I am the least of all the apostles. In fact, I'm not even worthy to be called an apostle after the way I persecuted God's church.*
> *10 But whatever I am now, it is all because God poured out his special favor on me—and not without results.*

What is true about Paul's story can be true for you and me. Jesus reveals himself to us, and we are adopted into this story.

Whether first hand, second hand or even thousands of years later, Jesus still shows us He is alive and saving us.

Let Us Pray

The Jesus Prayer
"Lord Jesus Christ, Son of God, have mercy on me a sinner."

The Lord's Prayer
Our Father who lives in heaven,
Holy is your name.
Your kingdom come, your will be done,
on earth as it is in heaven.
Give us this day our daily bread and forgive us our sins,
as we forgive those who sin against us.
Lead us not into temptation
but deliver us from evil.
For Yours is the Kingdom,
and the power and the glory
Forever. Amen

The Lord be with you today!

33

Preparing For Transition

Teach us to number our days that we may gain a heart of wisdom. Psalm 90:12 [Sunrise photo May 3 2013]

Day 33 Preparing For Transition

After his death, he presented himself alive to them in many different settings over a period of forty days. In face-to-face meetings, he talked to them about things concerning the kingdom of God. As they met and ate meals together, he told them ... Acts 1:2 (MSG)

The ascension will be here on Day 40, and Jesus will literally leave the scene.

Jesus was intentional about passing his mission on to his disciples, who were in turn to pass it on to others, and so on.

Nothing lasts forever in the natural world. The Jesus story affirms this. Even as the resurrected Lord, He knew He would be physically present for just 40 days.

Time is limited for all of us. If you're a leader (take a hint: worship leaders and pastors!) begin with the end in mind.

What would be the most empowering way to transition your mantle of leadership to the one following you? You have to prepare yourself, your successor and your people.

I've seen and experienced both good transitions and not-so-good transitions in leadership.

The good ones are purposeful, honorable and celebratory. The bad ones are awkward, not-well-thought-out, and painful.

Sometimes they've been a mixture of both. Messy comes with the territory. Be gracious.

Jesus knew he had 33 years to walk the planet, 3 years to do ministry, and 40 days to finish the job.

He was on a deadline.

Lord, teach us to number our days.

Let Us Pray

"Lord teach me to number my days, that I may gain a heart of wisdom (Psalm 90:12). Help me to empower those following me. Purify my heart and the work of my hands. Help to pass on only what is good and noble. In the name of the Father, Son and Holy Spirit, Amen."

34

Rest and Recreation

Jesus said, "let's take a break and get a little rest." Mark 6:30 [Sunrise May 4 2013, it was a rainy day and not the best photo op]

Day 34 Rest and Recreation

> *As they met and ate meals together, he told them that they were on no account to leave Jerusalem but **"must wait** for what the Father promised: the promise you heard from me. John baptized in water; you will be baptized in the Holy Spirit. And soon."* Acts 1:4-5 (MSG)

The truth is, as I write this, right now I could really use some R&R (rest and relaxation).

There is a biblical rhythm to work and rest – six days on, one day off.

> *"You have six days each week for your ordinary work, but on the seventh day you must stop working, even during the seasons of plowing and harvest."* Exodus 34:21 NLT

Sabbath rest is not optional, it's a commandment. Sadly, I find I break this one far too often. I gotta repent and change my ways. Again.

Active Waiting

In the Acts 1:4-5 passage I don't think Jesus was saying, "take a vacation" (although I wish I could interpret it that way!).

Rather, this was *active waiting,* a time of "constant prayer" (Acts 1:14) and intentionally *not* taking action until …

Until God was in it.

Jesus lived by this model of prayer and waiting. (*See:* Matthew 14:23; Mark 1:35; Luke 5:16).

The *Son of Man* practiced a rhythm of life that created space so he could hear clearly from his Heavenly Father.

Take a break

Jesus also *rested.* He was human and needed time to get his batteries recharged, just like you and me.

He instructed his followers to do the same.

> *The apostles then rendezvoused with Jesus and reported on all that they had done and taught. Jesus said,* ***"Come off by yourselves; let's take a break and get a little rest."*** *For there was constant coming and going. They didn't even have time to eat.* Mark 6:30-31 (MSG)

Have you had those days when you were so busy you couldn't even eat? I have, and Jesus did too. The way of wisdom was to stop and rest. Ok, let's do that.

Let Us Pray

I invite you to pray with me, if this is true for you too.

"Father I repent of not honoring your commandment to keep the Sabbath. Thank you for forgiving me. I trust your leadership to get the work done that needs to be done. Thank you for your faithfulness in all things. In Jesus name, Amen."

35

Seven Sundays of Easter

The Father is searching for those who worship him in Spirit and Truth. John 4:23

Day 35 The Seven Sundays of Easter

"The glory that you have given me I have given them, so that they may be one, as we are one." John 17: 22

I'm writing this chapter for the 6th Sunday of the Easter season.

In his book Ancient-Future Time Robert Webber states the *"essential theme of Easter cannot be communicated in a day. It takes a season."* In his chapter on Easter, he describes the practices of the ancient church to commemorate the season with the following emphasis.

1. **Easter Sunday.** Theme: Resurrection Sunday confirms the mission of God to restore all creation has been accomplished. Jesus is *Christus Victor,* "the one who destroys death and triumphed over the enemy and trampled Hades underfoot and bound the strong one, and carried off man to the heights of heaven." (Merlito of Sardid AD195)

2. **Second Sunday of Easter.** Theme: The Church understood as a community of people defined by resurrection spirituality.

3. **Third Sunday of Easter.** Theme: Worship: In worship resurrection spirituality is learned and experienced. "Do this in remembrance of me … "

4. **Fourth Sunday of Easter.** Theme: The Good Shepherd: We remember we follow the ultimate servant-leader, we listen to the voice of the Good Shepherd and follow his life.

5. **Fifth Sunday of Easter.** Theme: Ministry in the Church. The teaching emphasis shifts from explanation of the meaning of Christ's life, death and resurrection to preparation for Jesus' disciples to be the church, his body, as

the continued presence of Jesus in the world. The church itself is a sign of Jesus' resurrection.

6. **Sixth Sunday of Easter.** Theme: The Spirit. Ascension Day will happen on the following Thursday . According to Webber, baptism and the Eucharist are seen as signs of our union with God.

7. **Seventh Sunday of Easter.** Theme: The Prayer of Jesus (John 17) "The glory that you have given me I have given them, so that they may be one, as we are one" (John 17:22). The church is diverse but held together by the central fact that Jesus is the Son of God, he rose from the dead and is Lord of all.

8. **Pentecost Sunday.** Theme: The Holy Spirit coming with power and birthing the church.

God is into calendar.

If we bring a fresh heart to it, I believe seeking God in a focused way, aligned with patterns of the Christian calendar can be a beneficial practice of worship.

Why be random about it? You decide.

Let Us Pray

Our Father who lives in heaven, Holy is your name. Your Kingdom come, your will be done, on earth as it is in heaven. Give us this day our daily bread. Forgive us our sins, as we forgive those who sin against us. And lead us not into temptation, but deliver us from evil. For Yours is the Kingdom, and the power and the glory. Forever. Amen.

36

Tribe of The Like-Minded

Another rainy day and Monday. "Bless The Lord oh my soul!" Psalm 103 [Cloudy Sunrise May 6 2013]

Day 36 Tribe of The Like-Minded

They agreed they were in this for good, completely together in prayer .... there were about 120 of them in the room at the time
Acts 1:14-17 (MSG)

I had the honor recently of attending a gathering of worship dudes and dudettes from around the country. I've been to many worship-leader events, but I was awakened to the unique reason why this gathering felt like such a good fit.

It was a tribe of the like minded. A place where I felt like I *belonged.*

At the heart of any purposeful assembly of people are the elements of *chemistry and cohesion.*

When there is like-mindedness, everything just *works.*

By now, the followers of Jesus were catalyzed by their experiences with Christ. They had lived an unbelievable story. They had history together.

Yet they weren't gathered as a tribe just to remember the glory days.

Jesus had given them a follow through assignment, and it propelled them forward. They had to take action for a preferred future – to share the gospel with all nations.

Love for one another fueled their coalition of the willing.

Love was the only grid that made sense. And none of this made much sense.

They could encourage one another in this reality. "No, brother, you're not crazy. We saw and heard the same things, and we will serve the Lord together." And so they did.

Ministry, proclaiming the good news of the kingdom, was a group effort. We can't do it all alone.

It takes a tribe of the like-minded.

Let Us Pray

Lord thank you that I'm not alone. Thank you for like-minded brothers and sisters. Empower your people in every tribe to encourage one another to live the gospel. For Jesus sake. Amen.

The Lord be with you today!

37

Worship and Doubt

They worshiped him even though some doubted. Matthew 28:17 [Sunrise May 7 2013]

Day 37 Worship and Doubt

> *Then the eleven disciples left for Galilee, going to the mountain where Jesus had told them to go. ¹⁷ When they saw him, they worshiped him—but some of them doubted!* Matthew 28:16 (NLT)

Early in this devotional series we looked at the story of "doubting" Thomas (Many a Doubt: Day #4) and his response of worship ("My Lord and My God!" Day # 5).

In this passage from Matthew 28 we see the interaction of worship, faith and doubt.

Not all of those who experienced the truth of resurrection, whether by eye witness or first hand account, believed the same thing at the same time.

"Some doubted" and yet they worshiped him completely.

One understanding of "worship" is *human response to the divine revelation of God.*

Clearly the Messiah, as Matthew records, was adored wholeheartedly, even by those who still had twinges of doubt.

I'm like that. There are times I have more doubt than faith. How about you?

The good news is, Jesus said we only need a mustard seed of faith (Matthew 17:20). So, we take our doubt, we place it on the altar of the finished work of the cross, and offer that as a sacrifice of praise too.

When the pendulum of human reason swings more towards doubt than conviction, worship is more of a catalyst and less of a response. I believe choosing to worship while still having uncertainty actually *increases* faith and belief. What do you think? Would you agree with that idea?

Here's what other thinkers have to say about this passage in these commentary excerpts:

Worship

> *Worshipped (προσεκύνησαν) Prostrated themselves. The first time that the disciples are described as doing so.* – Vincent's Word Studies

> *With divine adoration, as the eternal Son of God; for so he was now declared to be by his resurrection from the dead,* – Gill's Exposition

> *They worshipped him – Paid him honour as the Messiah.* – Barnes Notes

Doubt

> *All that see the Lord Jesus with an eye of faith, will worship him. Yet the faith of the sincere may be very weak and wavering. But Christ gave such convincing proofs of his resurrection, as made their faith to triumph over doubts.* – Matthew Henry

> *The expression simply intimates, that they did not all believe at that time.* – Clarke's Commentary

> *But some doubted – As, for example, Thomas, John 20:25. The disciples had not expected his resurrection; they were therefore slow to believe. The mention of their doubting shows that they were honest men that they were not easily imposed on that they had not previously agreed to affirm that he had risen – that they were convinced only by the strength of the evidence. Their caution in examining the evidence; their slowness to believe; their firm conviction after all their doubts; and their willingness to show their conviction even by their "death," is most*

conclusive proof that they were "not" deceived in regard to the fact of his resurrection. – Barnes Notes on the Bible

May the spirit of God stir our hearts to worship and believe through every moment of doubt.

Let Us Pray

Jesus we worship and adore you as the Messiah, the promise of God fulfilled. Thank you that you are the Good Shepherd, and your sheep hear your voice. When all else seems unclear, may we hear the voice of the Master calling – "follow me". We love you. May your kingdom come , and your will be done, on earth as it is in heaven. In the name of the Father, the Son, and the Holy Spirit. Amen.

Be Still My Soul

>Be still, my soul: begin the song of praise
>On earth, believing, to Thy Lord on high;
>Acknowledge Him in all thy words and ways,
>So shall He view thee with a well pleased eye.
>Be still, my soul: the Sun of life divine
>Through passing clouds shall but more brightly shine.
>
>Words: Katharina A. von Schlegel, translation Jane L. Borthwick

38

All Authority

"Therefore go and make disciples of all the nations" Matthew 28:19 [Sunrise May 8 2013"]

Day 38 All Authority

^{18} Jesus came and told his disciples, "I have been given all authority in heaven and on earth. ^{19} Therefore, go and make disciples of all the nations, baptizing them in the name of the Father and the Son and the Holy Spirit. ^{20} Teach these new disciples to obey all the commands I have given you. And be sure of this: I am with you always, even to the end of the age."
Matthew 28:18-20 (NLT)

All authority (all power of rule) has been given to Me in heaven and on earth. (AMP)

Jesus is giving his followers a Great Commission that requires supernatural power, the kind that only comes from God. He assures them (and us!) that He has the the power and authority to not only command the assignment, but to empower them to accomplish it.

He is All Authority. Not only is He trustworthy, He is all powerful and able.

Paul describes the source of Christ's authority as coming from God in Philippians 2:9 " *God also has highly exalted him, and given him a name which is above every name:"*

The response of all creation to Christ's authority follows "*That at the name of Jesus every knee should bow, of things in heaven, and things in earth, and things under the earth; and that every tongue should confess that Jesus Christ is Lord, to the glory of God the Father."* (Philippians 2:10-11)

In the words of Charles Spurgeon "Power in the hands of some people is dangerous, but power in the hands of Christ is blessed. Oh, let him have all power! Let him do what he will with it, for he cannot will anything but that which is right, and just, and true, and good." Therefore;

- *We do not seek any other power.*
- *We defy every other power.*
- *We know our powerlessness will not hinder the progress of His kingdom.*
- *We give all our power unto Him.*

Our Commander-in-chief has authorized his followers to undertake a great mission. We can not do it on our own power, but by His power living in us.

Let Us Pray

Jesus tune our hearts to sing your praise. May we submit to Your authority before all others. Give us strength to do your will. May your kingdom come, and your will be done, on earth as it is in heaven. In the name of the Father, the Son, and the Holy Spirit. Amen.

39

He Ascended Into Heaven

Ascension Day: Jesus ascended into heaven and is seated at the right hand of the Father. Nicene Creed. [Sunrise May 9 2013]

Day 39 He ascended into heaven

> *⁹ After he said this, he was taken up before their very eyes, and a cloud hid him from their sight. ¹⁰ They were looking intently up into the sky as he was going, when suddenly two men dressed in white stood beside them. ¹¹ "Men of Galilee," they said, "why do you stand here looking into the sky? This same Jesus, who has been taken from you into heaven, will come back in the same way you have seen him go into heaven."* Acts 1:9-11 (NIV)

Ascension Day is traditionally observed on the Thursday 40 days after Resurrection Sunday, and 10 days before Pentecost Sunday. It commemorates the day Christ rose into heaven. Not a whole lot of protestant churches observe the Ascension, a fact lamented as "a great pity" by Robert Webber in Ancient-Future Time (p. 158)

The work of Jesus continues through his church, resurrection people empowered by the Holy Spirit. Jesus is present with his followers when they meet in His name.

> *"For where two or three gather in my name, there am I with them."* Matthew 18:20

Jesus is actively involved in our role of carrying out the Great Commission. He is positioned at the highest place of authority, the right hand of God the Father – clearing the way, helping us problem solve, and providing divine intervention on our behalf.

> *²⁵ Therefore He is able also to save to the uttermost (completely, perfectly, finally, and for all time and eternity) those who come to God through Him, since **He is always living to make petition to God and intercede with Him and intervene for them.*** Hebrews 7:25 (AMP)

One chapter has concluded. Another has just begun. The Ascension marks a closure to be celebrated with awe and wonder.

Lord I Lift Your Name On High

Lord I lift Your name on high
Lord I love to sing Your praises
I'm so glad You're in my life
I'm so glad You came to save us

You came from heaven to earth
To show the way
From the earth to the cross
My debt to pay
From the cross to the grave
From the grave to the sky
Lord I lift Your name on high

Rick Founds © 1989 Maranatha Praise, Inc. (Admin. by Maranatha! Music) CCLI Song # 117947

Let Us Pray

Lord I lift Your name on high. I am so glad you are in my life! Help me to be an ambassador for Christ today, in some small way. For the glory of the Father, the Son, and the Holy Spirit. Amen.

40

He's Coming Back!

Jesus is coming back. Acts 1:11 [Sunrise photo May 10 2013]

Day 40 He's coming back!

> ⁹⁻¹¹ These were his last words. As they watched, he was taken up and disappeared in a cloud. They stood there, staring into the empty sky. Suddenly two men appeared—in white robes! They said, "You Galileans!—why do you just stand here looking up at an empty sky? **This very Jesus who was taken up from among you to heaven will come as certainly—and mysteriously—as he left.**" Acts 1:9-11 (MSG)

I don't anticipate this truth as frequently or deeply as I should. Jesus is coming back, for sure – and not according to my expectations. The Kingdom of God will see *the return of the King.*

I heard Mike Bickle teaching at the One Thing Conference that our generation could possibly be seeing "the greatest worship movement in the history of the world."

That resonates with me. There has probably never been more worship going on the face of the earth than today. There has been an explosion of worship songs, worship music in the broadcast and internet media, and schools of worship training the next generation of leaders.

There has been a move of God that is transforming scores of just "regular people" to give themselves over to being *wholehearted worshipers.* That's what happened to me. Worship changed my life and ruined me for the ordinary.

The Holy Spirit is preparing the bride of Christ, His Church, for the bridegroom – *Jesus Christ.*

It is also true there has probably never been a more sinful era in the history of the world where so much moral perversion abounds. We live in the age of the wheat and tares (Matthew 13:24-30).

Those with discernment will read and heed the signs of the times. Certainly the church and the world is being prepared for the return of the Lord.

Live and act accordingly.

Honor and Majesty

> Part 2 (Chorus)

Let the heavens be glad and the earth rejoice
Let the seas resound with a mighty roar
Let the trees and the fields shout a song of joy
For He's coming again, yes He's coming again
Oh He's coming again, yes He's coming again

In all His honor and majesty

> Rob Still © 2001/2011 Rob Still Music CCLI Song # 117947

Let Us Pray

I invite you to pray with me.

Lord awaken my heart to be ready. Stir up my thinking and realign my priorities. Help me to not only be prepared, but like the forerunner, help me be one who prepares the way of the Lord for others. For the glory of the Father, the Son, and the Holy Spirit. Amen.

41

Timing Is God's Business

"Timing is the Father's business" Acts1:7
[Not much of a sunrise today. Photo May 11 2013]

Day 41 Timing Is God's Business

> ^{6} *When they were together for the last time they asked, "Master, are you going to restore the kingdom to Israel now? Is this the time?"*
>
> $^{7\text{-}8}$ *He told them, "You don't get to know the time.* **Timing is the Father's business.** *What you'll get is the Holy Spirit. And when the Holy Spirit comes on you, you will be able to be my witnesses in Jerusalem, all over Judea and Samaria, even to the ends of the world." Acts 1:6-8 (MSG)*

Imagine this scene as Jesus is giving his very last words. In the preceding 40 something days his followers had lived through the most unbelievable, miraculous moments in history.

Now they asked a legit question. "Lord, what's the plan? Are the rest of the prophecies going to be fulfilled now?"

And Jesus says, "Sorry, I can't tell you that. You still have to go on and do the next right thing by faith."

Trust in God is the only currency we have as believers. It will be tested and tried to the breaking point and beyond. Jesus did not say, "everything is going to be ok now."

> *... when the Son of Man comes, will he find faith on the earth?" Luke 18:8*

I do not have faith that everything on this side of heaven is going to work out "ok". I have faith that God will work all things together for good (Romans 8:28).

There is a difference.

When the Holy Spirit "comes on you" it *transforms* you.

The same power that gave every first generation disciple *the courage to die rather than lie* is here today for you and me.

The timing of God's justice is His business.

God Is In Control

Anybody remember the Twila Paris song "God is In Control" ? It was S*ong of the Year* back in 1995.

> God is in control
> We believe that His children will not be forsaken
> God is in control
> We will choose to remember and never be shaken
> There is no power above or beside Him, we know
> Oh, God is in control, oh God is in control

Let Us Pray

Lord , I agree with the truth of Your Word, that You are good and your love endures forever! So often the evil and cruelty of this world seems to mock this truth. Fill me fresh with your Holy Spirit to live for your glory, no matter the circumstance. In the name of the Father, the Son, and the Holy Spirit. Amen.

42

From Tribe to Family

Whoever does the will of God is my brother and sister and mother. Mark 3:35 [Sunrise May 12 2013]

Day 42 From Tribe to Family

> "*All of these with their minds in full agreement devoted themselves steadfastly to prayer, [waiting together] with the women and **Mary the mother of Jesus, and with His brothers.**"*
> Acts 1:14 (AMP)

During the ten day period between the ascension of Jesus and the outpouring of the Holy Spirit, his followers became more than a tribe, they became a family. The core group were his eleven disciples plus "the women", joined by his natural family – mother Mary and his brothers.

A tribe is a collective of the like-minded. Now they decided they were all-in. They grew deeper. They progressed from *agreement to commitment*. "They agreed they were in this for good" (Acts 1:14 MSG)

As we grow closer to the Lord, we grow closer to one another. The fruit of intimacy is more intimacy. A deep trust develops and is sustained. Growth is what happens when people are healed and healthy.

Jesus had redefined "family", and they became one.

> "*Whoever does God's will is my brother and sister and mother.*" Mark 3:35

They must have appeared as fanatics to outsiders.

An amazing turnaround in Jesus family had occurred. At one time his family "thought him insane" (Mark 3:21) and tried to stop his craziness. I guess witnessing your brother's crucifixion and resurrection will change your perspective.

Jesus was often misunderstood and rejected, but that never stopped Him from doing the will of the Father.

Let Us Pray

Jesus, you blessed your earthly mother. May we do the same, and in the same humility of spirit. Heal our natural families. Heal your church that gathers in your name. May your kingdom come , and your will be done. In the name of the Father, the Son, and the Holy Spirit. Amen.

43

Living Water!

Let all the thirsty come! John 7:37-39 [Sunrise pic May 13 2013]

Day 43 Living Water!

For John baptized with water, but not many days from now you shall be baptized with (placed in, introduced into) the Holy Spirit. Acts 1:5 (AMP)

Jesus was at the finish line of his run on earth. Moments before his ascension he promised the Holy Spirit was coming soon.

Earlier in his ministry he was very bold to confront the religious system. He "spoke life" prophetically at the temple by declaring in a loud voice:

^{37} On the last day, the climax of the festival, Jesus stood and shouted to the crowds,

"Anyone who is thirsty may come to me!

^{38} Anyone who believes in me may come and drink!

For the Scriptures declare, 'Rivers of living water will flow from his heart.'"

^{39} (When he said "living water," he was speaking of the Spirit, who would be given to everyone believing in him. But the Spirit had not yet been given, because Jesus had not yet entered into his glory.) John 7:37-39

Now that promise was being fulfilled. Jesus was entering his glory, and the Spirit was soon to be given.

Let All The Thirsty Come

This idea of "living water" has been a powerful inspiration to me for many years. *"Jesus is the living water springing up in me."*

Back in the day at Belmont Church, one of our favorite songs was **"Let All the Thirsty Come"** composed by John G. Elliott, along with Amy Grant, based on John 7:37-39

I didn't personally know John at that time, but in his role as worship leader, he was one of my first mentors in experiencing worship. I'm privileged to know him now as a friend and colleague.

Over the years, there were countless hours our family worshiped with his CDs at home or in the car. This song is a classic.

Let all the thirsty come
Let all the hungry come
Let all who seek for living water
Find it in the Son

The angels sing His name
And I will do the same
For drawing near to Him
We'll find Him drawing closer by
Lift up the Lord on high
And surely we will find
The bread of heaven fall
And living water for us all
Filling our hearts

The bread of life is free
To meet my deepest need
And Jesus is the living water
Springing up in me

Amy Grant | John G. Elliott
© 1990 Age To Age Music, Inc., BMG Songs, Inc., Pamela Kay Music (Admin. by EMI Christian Music Publishing), Riverstone Music, Inc.

Let Us Pray:

Come thou fount of every blessing, tune my heart to sing your praise! Jesus fill me today and everyday with Your living waters. Fill me with your love, joy, peace, faithfulness, goodness, gentleness and self-control. Thank you that we are blessed to be a blessing. May your kingdom come, and your will be done, on earth as it is in heaven. For your glory alone. In the name of the Father, the Son, and the Holy Spirit. Amen.

44

How God Chooses Leaders

People look at the outward appearance but the Lord looks at the heart. 1 Samuel 16:7 [Sunrise photo May 14 2013]

Day 44 How God Chooses Leaders

> ^{23} *So they nominated two men: Joseph called Barsabbas (also known as Justus) and Matthias.* ^{24} *Then they all prayed, "O Lord, you know every heart. Show us which of these men you have chosen* ^{25} *as an apostle to replace Judas in this ministry, for he has deserted us and gone where he belongs."* ^{26} *Then they cast lots, and Matthias was selected to become an apostle with the other eleven. Acts 1:23-26* (NLT)

The truth is, I don't exactly know *how* God chooses leaders. Do you?

Here's what I've seen over years of personal experience, along with studying Biblical examples. There are a wide range of methods and criteria that God uses to choose leaders. Some are born into it (John the Baptist, Solomon), some are groomed for it (Joshua and Elisha), some are suddenly called and life radically interrupted (most of the disciples, Paul), many are reluctant (Moses and Gideon), some just seemed destined for it (David).

God does what He does and chooses who He chooses for reasons only He fully knows. Only God truly knows anyone's heart. But the Lord can only work with those who have the right kind of heart. This is most important.

Leaders Solve Problems

So in the **"Matthias Replaces Judas"** story (Acts 1:12-26), Peter steps up as a leader. He presents a problem to the group's attention. This is what leaders do, they look to the future and chart a course.

Peter points out that the leadership role of the 12th disciple is important practically and Biblically. In verse 20 he interprets Psalm 69:25 and Psalm 109:8 as giving prophetic direction for Judas to be replaced.

The disciples agree to make a decision. Then they sought the Lord with an open mind. This had to be a God choice, not the fixed-result of a political "good-ol-boy" system.

> *⁴ Then they all prayed, "O Lord, you know every heart. Show us which of these men you have chosen."*

This is the mindset for a group to have when charged with choosing leaders. Get God's heart on the matter.

The next move seems quite odd by our cultural understanding. They cast lots. Seems pretty random.

This must have been a win / win choice, both guys were equally qualified and either would have done a great job.

Honestly, I personally can't recommend tossing a coin, but hey what do I know? God's ways are not my ways.

And that's the point.

Winning The Lottery

Mattias won the lottery, Justus did not. They both had the same mission, just different roles.

They both had to accept the decision as being God's will, move on, and seek to serve God's dream – to share the good news.

Probably Mattias had the more prestigious role, he was now one of the inner circle, Justus was not.

Mattias had to trust God and guard his heart against pride. I'm sure he was a quality guy of character and the Lord could trust him in this assignment.

Justus had to trust God and guard his heart against feeling rejected and maybe angry. I'm sure he was a quality guy of character and the Lord could trust him in a different assignment.

May we accept God's ways and decisions with the same degree of trust.

Let Us Pray

It's a good day for the Lord's Prayer in the old English.

Our Father who art in heaven, hallowed be thy name. Thy Kingdom come, Thy will be done, on earth as it is in heaven. Give us this day our daily bread. And forgive us our trespasses, as we forgive those who trespass against us. Lead us not into temptation, but deliver us from evil. For thine is the Kingdom and the power and the glory. Forever. Amen.

45

Lo, I Am With You Always

"And lo, I am with you always, even to the end of the age" Matthew 28:20
[Sunrise Photo May 15 2013]

Day 45 Lo, I am with you always...

> *18 And Jesus came and spoke to them, saying, "All authority has been given to Me in heaven and on earth. 19 Go therefore and make disciples of all the nations, baptizing them in the name of the Father and of the Son and of the Holy Spirit, 20 teaching them to observe all things that I have commanded you;* **and lo, I am with you always, even to the end of the age."** *Amen.* Matthew 28:18-20

These are the very last words of Jesus recorded by Matthew. This scripture has been a great comfort to me, as I'm sure it was to his disciples. He transferred leadership of his mission to his successors, as unlikely as they were.

The presence of Christ, his Spirit – the Holy Spirit, would be with them, to give them hope and courage. And Jesus promises to do that for us today.

We are not in this life, this mission, this fight, this journey, this story – alone. To all who believe, Jesus is right there beside us, "guarding, guiding all the way."

> *Yea, though I walk through the valley of the shadow of death,*
> *I will fear no evil;*
> *For You are with me;*
> *Your rod and Your staff, they comfort me.* Psalm 23:4

Jesus Son of God, articulates the heart of God the Father, who promises to *"never leave thee nor forsake thee."*

> *"Be strong and courageous. Do not be afraid or terrified because of them, for the LORD your God goes with you; he will never leave you nor forsake you."* Deuteronomy 31:6 (Moses commission to Joshua)

The presence of Jesus will be with us forever – til the end of all time. Until the end of the world as we know it.

"I'll be with you as you do this, day after day after day, right up to the end of the age." The Message

Let Us Pray

Today's prayer is an excerpt from Adam Clarke's [1831] Bible Commentary at the end of Matthew. I invite you to pray with me.

May the Divine Author of this sacred book give the reader a heartfelt experience of all the truths it contains; make and keep him wise unto salvation; build him up in this most holy faith; and give him an inheritance among the blessed, through Christ Jesus, the Friend of mankind, and the Savior of sinners, who is the object and end of this glorious system of truth! And to Him, with the Father and Eternal Spirit, be glory and dominion, thanksgiving and obedience, for ever and ever, Amen and amen!

46

Signs, Wonders, and Miracles

Blessed are those who fear the Lord, who find great delight in Him! Psalm 112:1 [Sunrise May 16 2013]

Day 46 Signs, Wonders and Miracles

*ⁱ⁵ He said to them, "Go into all the world and preach the gospel to all creation. ¹⁶ Whoever believes and is baptized will be saved, but whoever does not believe will be condemned. ¹⁷ **And these signs will accompany those who believe:** In my name they will drive out demons; they will speak in new tongues; ¹⁸ they will pick up snakes with their hands; and when they drink deadly poison, it will not hurt them at all; they will place their hands on sick people, and they will get well." Mark 16:15-18* (NIV)

The signs that Jesus says will accompany those who believe is pretty radical stuff.

- Driving out demons
- Speaking in new tongues
- Picking up snakes (*Say what?* But that's what it says!)
- Drink poison with no ill effects
- Heal the sick by the laying on of hands

Although this may seem fantastic and unbelievable, all these signs are recorded as being fulfilled in the historical record. And I have personally witnessed some of these signs myself.

We worship a *supernatural* God, afterall, not a religious cultural institution.

The record shows that *"through the hands of the apostles many signs and wonders were done among the people." Acts 5:12*

Here's a breakdown:

- **Driving out demons**

    - Acts 16:18, Paul cast out the spirit of divination from the fortune-teller girl
    - *"Many evil spirits were cast out, screaming as they left their victims. And many who had been paralyzed or lame were healed."* Acts 8:7 (KJV)
    - "They shall cast out devils"; this power was more common among Christians than any other, and lasted longer, as appears by the testimonies of Justin Martyr, Origen, Irenaeus, Tertullian Minutius Felix, and others, cited by Grotius on this place. [Matthew Henry Commentary]
    - I think I have personally seen this.

- **Speaking in new tongues (or languages)**

    - This was remarkably fulfilled on the day of Pentecost, Acts 2:4-11. It existed, also, in other places. See 1 Corinthians 12:10. [Barnes Commentary]
    - I know I have personally seen this.

- **Picking up snakes** (*Say what?* But that's what it says!)

    - "They shall take up serpents." This was fulfilled in Paul, who was not hurt by the viper that fastened on his hand, which was acknowledged a great miracle by the barbarous people, Acts 28:5, 6. They shall be kept unhurt by that generation of vipers among

whom they live, and by the malice of the old serpent. [Matthew Henry Commentary]
- I have *not* personally seen this.

- **Drink poison with no ill effects**

  - If they be compelled by their persecutors to drink any deadly poisonous thing, it shall not hurt them: of which very thing some instances are found in ecclesiastical history. [Matthew Henry Commentary]
  - I have *not* personally seen this.

- **Heal the sick**

  - *"... and many who had been paralyzed or lame were healed."* "Acts 8:7 (KJV)
  - Peter and John heal the lame man Acts 3:1-8
  - Acts 9:32 Peter raises Dorca from the dead
  - Many of the elders of the church had this power, as appears by Jam. 5:14, where, as an instituted sign of this miraculous healing, they are said to anoint the sick with oil in the name of the Lord. [Matthew Henry Commentary]
  - I know I have personally seen and experienced this more than once, glory to God.

Hebrews 13:8 proclaims that Jesus is the same , yesterday, today and forever.

I believe that. How about you?

What He promised yesterday – He still promises today. ***These signs will accompany those who believe!***

> *Jesus Christ (the Messiah) is [always] the same, yesterday, today, [yes] and forever (to the ages).* Hebrews 13:8 (AMP)

Let Us Pray

I invite you to pray with me.

Lord, let faith rise up in all who read your Word. May we be anointed to share the good news to all creation. Jesus saves. Jesus heals. Jesus delivers. In the name of the Father, the Son and the Holy Spirit. Amen.

47

Pour Out Your Spirit Lord!

Pour out your Spirit Lord, on your people! (c) Tom Lane [Sunrise photo May 1/ 2013]

Day 47 Pour Out Your Spirit Lord

As I write this, Pentecost Sunday is just a few days away. This is the day the church was birthed, with a dramatic and spectacular manifestation of the Holy Spirit, unlike anything ever known before on earth.

The audio track must have been deafening, a sound from heaven, like a tornado – a mighty roaring violent wind. The tongues of fire, the ecstatic cacophony of every language declaring the wonders of God – all this drew a quite a crowd, and the audience was blown away, utterly "thunderstruck" (MSG).

"Amazed and perplexed they asked one another, 'What does this mean?" Acts 2:12

That's the million dollar question.

Peter, inspired by the Holy Spirit, starts talking. Now the Great Commission is launched.

The disciples had followed Jesus wholeheartedly during his ministry, they had experienced an additional 40 days with him after his resurrection, then they had waited on the Lord in prayer for another 10 days …

The next move in God's cosmic plan culminated in this explosive moment. It was beyond nuclear.

"What does this mean?"

Peter put it all together.

Peter Preaches to the Crowd

> [14] Then Peter stepped forward with the eleven other apostles and shouted to the crowd, "Listen carefully, all of you, fellow Jews

and residents of Jerusalem! Make no mistake about this. [15] These people are not drunk, as some of you are assuming. Nine o'clock in the morning is much too early for that. [16] No, what you see was predicted long ago by the prophet Joel:

[17] 'In the last days,' God says,
'I will pour out my Spirit upon all people.
Your sons and daughters will prophesy.
Your young men will see visions,
and your old men will dream dreams.

[18] In those days I will pour out my Spirit
even on my servants—men and women alike—
and they will prophesy.

[19] And I will cause wonders in the heavens above
and signs on the earth below—
blood and fire and clouds of smoke.

[20] The sun will become dark,
and the moon will turn blood red
before that great and glorious day of the Lord arrives.

[21] And everyone who calls on the name of the Lord
will be saved.' Acts 2:14-21 (NLT)

This was the sign of the fulfillment of God's prophetic promises, with the ultimate purpose of salvation. The mission of proclaiming the gospel was now assigned to his church.

> *[9] The Lord is not slack concerning his promise, as some men count slackness; but is longsuffering to us-ward,* **not willing that any should perish, but that all should come to repentance. 2 Peter 3:9**

Friends, I pray that the magnificence of Pentecost is remembered and perpetuated in our worship this weekend.

Let Us Pray

Almighty God, on this day you opened the way of eternal life to every race and nation by the promised gift of your Holy Spirit.*   Fill your church with power, kindle flaming hearts within us, and cause us to proclaim your mighty works in every tongue, that all may call on you and be saved,** through Jesus Christ our Lord, who lives and reigns with you, in the unity of the Holy Spirit, one God, for ever and ever. Amen.*

[A combination of Pentecost prayers from *Scot McNight and **Lawrence Stookey UMC #542]

Here's great song of intercession by my friend Tom Lane.

Pour Out Your Spirit Lord

Verse 1
Pour out Your Spirit Lord on Your people (3x)
Let it reign let it reign
Verse 2
Pour out Your mercy Lord on Your people (3x)
Let it reign let it reign
BRIDGE
Turn the hearts of fathers to their children
And ev'ry nation to the God of love and holiness
Let the fire of Your Spirit burn
Verse 3
Pour out Your fire Lord on Your people (3x)
Let it reign let it reign

Tom Lane
© 1999 The Bridge Worx , worshiptogether.com songs

48

Visions and Dreams

Sons and daughters, prophesy. Young men, visions. Old men, dreams. Acts 2:17 [Sunrise May 18 2013]

Day 48 Visions and Dreams

The day of Pentecost. All heaven is breaking loose. People are astounded and wondering – *"what is going on?"*

Peter explains the events of that first Pentecost moment. Connecting the prophetic dots he quotes Joel 2:28.

> *"In the last days, God says, I will pour out my Spirit on all people. Your sons and daughters will prophesy, your young men will see visions, your old men will dream dreams." Acts 2:17* (NIV)

I'm in my early 50's as I write this, an "old man" by biblical standards. *(I'm in denial, most days I feel much younger!)*

This whole idea of prophecy, visions and dreams is about **seeing a better future.**

God has a dream, it is for union with his creation. God is all about relationship, and restoring what has been lost.

> *I will take you as my own people, and I will be your*
> *God.* Exodus 6:7

We need a vision to see what God sees. We need to dream God's dream.

Whatever your future course, does it lead you and others closer to God – *or not?*

God takes the initiative and pours out His spirit on everyone who is saved regardless of race, gender, position – all humanity.

This outpouring is for the proclamation of the gospel, for building the KIngdom of God.

From the overflow of His Spirit inside each of us, we get God's vision and God's dream of specific destinations and action steps to get there.

John Wesley's commentary has an interesting insight on this passage:

> 2:17 The times of the Messiah are frequently called the last days, the Gospel being the last dispensation of Divine grace. I will pour out of my Spirit – Not on the day of pentecost only, upon all flesh – On persons of every age, sex, and rank. And your young men shall see visions – In young men the outward sense, are most vigorous, and the bodily strength is entire, whereby they are best qualified to sustain the shock which usually attends the visions of God. In old men the internal senses are most vigorous, suited to divine dreams. Not that the old are wholly excluded from the former, nor the young from the latter.

God's plan has a role for every generation, in every season of life. A place for the energy of the younger, and a role for the wisdom of the older.

Dream Big!

Let Us Pray:

Almighty God, on this day you opened the way of eternal life to every race and nation by the promised gift of your Holy Spirit.* Fill your church with power, kindle flaming hearts within us, and cause us to proclaim your mighty works in every tongue, that all may call on you and be saved,** through Jesus Christ our Lord, who lives and reigns with you, in the unity of the Holy Spirit, one God, for ever and ever. Amen.* [Prayer sources: *Scot McNight, **Lawrence Stookey UMC #542]

49

The Significance of Pentecost

May every tongue declare the wonders of God! (see Acts 2:11) [Sunrise photo: Archives 3-15-13]

Day 49 The Significance of Pentecost

When the Feast of Pentecost came, they were all together in one place. Without warning there was a sound like a strong wind, gale force—no one could tell where it came from. It filled the whole building. Then, like a wildfire, the Holy Spirit spread through their ranks, and they started speaking in a number of different languages as the Spirit prompted them. Acts 2:1-4 (MSG)

This is the Sunday we remember the coming of the Holy Spirit, the birth of the Church.

This chapter in God's story is as significant as the Creation, when God created the heavens and the earth; the Incarnation, when God became a man; and Redemption, when Christ atoned for the sins of the world.

Now the work of Recreation is fully released – through Christ we can be new creations, all things are made new.

> *"Broadly speaking Pentecost brings understanding to the followers of Jesus, empowers them in ministry, establishes the church, and points to the end of history when the kingdom of Christ will be established over all the earth."*
> Robert E. Webber Ancient-Future Time (p. 161)

So … The Lord be with you! Celebrate Pentecost.

The Nicene Creed

We believe in one God,
the Father, the Almighty,
maker of heaven and earth,
of all that is, seen and unseen.

We believe in one Lord, Jesus Christ,
the only Son of God,
eternally begotten of the Father,
God from God, Light from Light,
true God from true God,
begotten, not made,
of one Being with the Father.
Through him all things were made.
For us and for our salvation
he came down from heaven:
by the power of the Holy Spirit
he became incarnate from the Virgin Mary,
and was made man.
For our sake he was crucified under Pontius Pilate;
he suffered death and was buried.
On the third day he rose again
in accordance with the Scriptures;
he ascended into heaven
and is seated at the right hand of the Father.
He will come again in glory to judge the living and the dead,
and his kingdom will have no end.

We believe in the Holy Spirit, the Lord, the giver of life,
who proceeds from the Father and the Son.
With the Father and the Son he is worshiped and glorified.
He has spoken through the Prophets.
We believe in one holy catholic and apostolic Church.
We acknowledge one baptism for the forgiveness of sins.
We look for the resurrection of the dead,
and the life of the world to come. Amen.

—Episcopal Church *Book of Common Prayer* (1979), *The Book of Common Prayer*.

Let Us Pray:

Almighty God, on this day you opened the way of eternal life to every race and nation by the promised gift of your Holy Spirit.* Fill your church with power, kindle flaming hearts within us, and cause us to proclaim your mighty works in every tongue, that all may call on you and be saved,** through Jesus Christ our Lord, who lives and reigns with you, in the unity of the Holy Spirit, one God, for ever and ever. Amen.* [Prayer sources: *Scot McNight; **Lawrence Stookey UMC #542]

50

Joy Is The Secret Sauce

You show the way of life, you fill me with the joy of your presence. Acts 2:28
[Sunrise May 20 2013]

Day 50 Joy Is The Secret Sauce

³² "God raised Jesus from the dead, and we are all witnesses of this. ³³ Now he is exalted to the place of highest honor in heaven, at God's right hand. And the Father, as he had promised, gave him the Holy Spirit to pour out upon us, just as you see and hear today." Acts 2:32-33

Who is Jesus?

At Pentecost, the Holy Spirit released fresh revelation of exactly who Jesus was and helped make sense of what God was doing.

Peter's spontaneous sermon was inspired by the Spirit filling him, and everyone present, with an unprecedented level of divine insight.

During his earthly ministry, the identity of *Jesus as God* was not obvious to all. Even when Jesus was there in the flesh living and talking with them, they often didn't get what He was talking about. And some rejected Jesus even when it was plain He *had to be* the promised Messiah.

This whole thing is mind blowing when you think about it.

Joy

In this first gospel proclamation, Peter quotes David from Psalm 16:11.

> *You have shown me the way of life, and you will fill me with the joy of your presence. Acts 2: 28*

Here, I believe, is what is intrinsically attractive about the gospel, about following Jesus Christ as Lord and Master.

Jesus shows us the "way of life" and fills us with joy. He came that we might have a life full of abundance (John 10:10). God's heart is generous to bless his children.

Jesus fills the huge gap we all have in the human experience, namely, finding true meaning and joy in this earthly existence.

"Religion", understood as doing "the right things" just doesn't cut it. Neither does "success" – attaining a degree of money, power, prestige. Nor does the pursuit of "pleasure" – doing whatever feels good when you feel like doing it.

These are the means people employ to experience joy, pursuing happiness by the logic of human nature. It is folly.

The followers of Jesus discovered something far superior, they were filled with *joy in his presence.*

My friends, *the joy of His presence* is the secret sauce of a life in God.

Joy is the benefit of worshiping Father, Son and Holy Spirit in *sprit and truth.*

Transformation

This group in the Upper Room, these *resurrection witnesses* – were not motivated by pressure, coercion, guilt trips or any other mechanism of man.

In the presence of Jesus they found love, joy, peace, hope. Their passion was *real.*

They had been transformed.

Inspired by and motivated by supernatural love, they shared their stories of how Jesus had changed their lives. *Nothing could stop them!*

And that's what proclaiming the gospel is – telling your God story, and leading others to enjoy the wonderful truth of knowing Him personally.

May the joy of the Lord be your strength today, and always!

Let Us Pray:

"Jesus thank you for your life, your death and your resurrection. Thank you for sending your Holy Spirit. Fill me with your Spirit today. Fill me with a new anointing, a fresh outpouring. Thank you for the joy of your presence. Empower me to do Your work, Your way. For the glory of the Father, the Son and the Holy Spirit. Amen."

51

Epilogue: Where Do We Go From Here?

And all the believers lived in a wonderful harmony....Acts 2:44 [Sunrise May 22 2013]

Epilogue: Where Do We Go From Here?

> *⁴³ A deep sense of awe came over them all, and the apostles performed many miraculous signs and wonders. ⁴⁴ And all the believers lived in a wonderful harmony, and shared everything they had. ⁴⁵ They sold their property and possessions and shared the money with those in need. ⁴⁶ They worshiped together at the Temple each day, met in homes for the Lord's Supper, and shared their meals with great joy and generosity - every meal a celebration, exuberant and joyful, ⁴⁷ all the while praising God and enjoying the goodwill of all the people. People in general liked what they saw. And each day the Lord added to their fellowship those who were being saved. Acts 2:43-47 (NLT / MSG)*

We began this series the day after Resurrection Sunday with the question, *Now What?*

Now 50 plus days later, and after the spectacular outpouring of the Holy Spirit on Pentecost Sunday, we ask – *"Where do we go from here?"*

This passage from Acts 2:44-47 describes the next move of the believers who were living it in real time.

They embraced a completely new, counter culture lifestyle.

Here we get a glimpse of what Christian community could and should look like. And for a brief window of time, it's beautiful.

I remain an idealist for the possibilities of Christian community, despite all the garbage of church history and the baggage of modern day *church-ian-ity*.

What if we could live going forward in that same spirit of fresh revelation? What does a transformed community look like? How is the church supposed to represent Christ?

Acts 2 shows the first fruits of Christian community were:

- Reverence, awe and respect for who God is, and what He was and *is* doing
- Powerful demonstrations of God's love released through the believers
- Harmony amongst all the community
- Generosity from and for all
- Worship that is celebratory, exuberant and joyful
- Praise that is attractive and God centered
- Joy
- Favor amongst all people
- Growth and increase

This was the model of a happy, wholehearted, worshiping community.

Encouraging *wholehearted worship* has been my heart's desire – my passion and my mission, for a long time now. But what I've learned through my journey, is that a "worship leader" is actually quite limited. He or she can neither coax nor produce authentic, wholehearted *worship.*

Only the presence of God can woo the human spirit to respond in genuine adoration. Only the power of God Almighty through Jesus Christ can heal, restore and renew each of us from our broken, lost and ignorant condition.

He takes our shattered hearts and makes them whole. He takes our brief lifetimes and makes them significant.

Our response to the work of God in our lives is *worship*.

May the Lord bless you as you read this. May He release a fresh revelation and outpouring of His presence in every aspect of your life.

May we all be transformed as those first friends of Jesus, and may we bear the fruit of God's Holy Spirit changing us for His glory.

The Lord be with you! Worship Him!

Let's Pray:

I invite you to pray with me. Today's prayer is a benediction from Colossians 3:15-17

> *May the peace of Christ rule in your hearts,*
> *to which indeed you were called in one body;*
> *and be thankful.*
>
> *May the word of Christ richly dwell within you,*
> *with all wisdom teaching and admonishing one another*
> *with psalms and hymns and spiritual songs,*
> *singing with thankfulness in your hearts to God.*
>
> *And whatever you do in word or deed,*
> *do all in the name of the Lord Jesus,*
> *giving thanks through Him to God the Father.*
>
> *Amen.*

Bonus Resources

Thank you for reading!

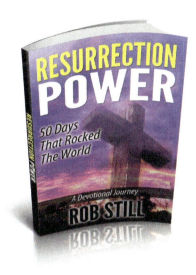

We've got free bonuses for you at

Resurrection Power Book Club

http://www.robstill.com/ressurection-power-book-club/

The password is: resurrection power

Also, More Free Resources For Worship at

robstill.com

About The Author

Rob Still is a worship leader, songwriter, and producer in Nashville TN. He is on a mission to *"encourage wholehearted worship worldwide",* teaching at workshops and conferences throughout North America and on the mission field in eastern Europe, Latin America, Asia and Africa. He blogs and offers free worship resources at RobStill.com.

He has a Masters Degree in Worship Studies from the Robert E. Webber Institute for Worship Studies. On the mission field, Rob has been the Director of Worship for the Sozo International Music & Arts Festival in Eastern Europe and instructor of "Practical Theology of Worship" at the Scoala de Inchinare (School of Worship) in Timisoara, Romania.

He is the Director of Music and Worship at Hendersonville First United Methodist Church, where he helped launch the contemporary worship ministry. Previously he served as Pastor of Worship and Arts at Music Row's Belmont Church, Nashville TN, overseeing a ministry of over 250 musicians, singers, and worship leaders. He has led youth worship for many years and was founder of the *Rock-n-Worship Youth Band Camp.*

His songs have been featured in Worship Leader Magazine's SongDiscovery series and are published by worshiptogether.com/ EMI Christian Music Group. His music projects "What Words Can't Say", "The Forerunner" and "A Friend of John's" are available on Amazon.com and I-Tunes.

An award winning music producer, Rob produced jingles and post-scores for advertising clients including Wal-Mart, Nike, Texaco, FEMA, Pizza Hut, Cracker Barrel and hundreds of national brands.

Here's how to stay connected with Rob Still:

Website: http://robstill.com
Twitter: @robstill
Facebook: rob.still.1
Facebook Page: Encouraging-Wholehearted-Worship-Rob-Still
Email: rob@robstill.com

Music By Rob Still

MUSIC AVAILABLE ON AMAZON.COM *and* I-TUNES

WHAT WORDS CAN'T SAY **Featuring:** *What Words Can't Say, Honor & Majesty, Never Alone, No Easy Answers*

The Forerunner + a Friend of John's (Double Cd)
Featuring: A New Anointing, The Jesus La La Song, Faithful

About Our Missions Work

Rob Still Ministries, Inc is the non-profit organization set up to fund our international missions work.

We consider it an honor to share the good news of Jesus Christ throughout the world. People are hungry for the the truth and liberation of of the gospel.

The purpose of *Rob Still Ministries* is to proclaim the good news of Jesus Christ internationally. We do this through **short-term missions trips** to under-resourced areas of the world.

For over 14 years we have served extensively in the formerly Communist countries of **Eastern Europe,** particularly *Romania, Hungary, and Serbia.* We have also ministered in Argentina, Mexico,

Guatemala, Ecuador, the Caribbean, The Philippines, Germany, England, The Netherlands, Poland, and other nations.

What We Do

We invest in the nations by going and making **disciples.** We do this by teaching biblical foundations of Christian worship. We teach about worship, music, leadership and life. We encourage wholehearted worship worldwide by helping people understand specifically their identity and destiny in Christ. We also donate musical instruments, musical supplies, books and worship resources.

My Story As *"One Who Goes"*

In 1997 I was invited to go on a short term missions trip to the Philippines. I felt the Lord say, *"if you go, it will change your life."* I was 37 and it was my first time out of the country. My role was to teach on songwriting and worship leading. We had a ministry team of about 12 people. We did worship events everywhere and held classes in the cities and the jungles. It was incredible.

My next missions trip was in 2001 to the *Sozo Festival* in Hungary. The following year 2002, things accelerated. I returned to Hungary, then traveled to Argentina with *Musico a Musico*. There was an amazing revival going on there. These experiences, and the many that followed, gave me a glimpse of *"every nation, every language, every tribe, every tongue"* wholeheartedly, passionately, radically worshiping God.

After that I felt the call of God to **go back to school**, get my *Masters Degree in Worship Studies*, and be one of those who goes and makes disciples. Now I've taught in over 20 nations about worship, theology and songwriting.

I'm using the term "we" and "I" interchangeably because, although I have done most of the missions travel, my super awesome wife **Ivalene** has also been a significant contributor in our missions work.

Ivalene is *excellent* teaching children's music and has served several times as director of the Children's School of Worship seminar at the Sozo Festival.

Partner With Us.

We invite you to pray about partnering with us. Sign up for my newsletter and find out more about our latest missions trips at **robstillministries.org** and **robstill.com/missions**.

*Here I am, send me! (*Isaiah 6:8)

Help fulfill the Great Commission by supporting our missions work. Donations are tax deductible and can be made on-line at robstillministries.org. ***Rob Still Ministries, Inc*** is a Tennessee Non-Profit Corporation and 501(c)(3) charity organized exclusively for charitable, religious, and educational purposes.

CPSIA information can be obtained
at www.ICGtesting.com
Printed in the USA
LVOW02s1933250417
532178LV00005B/8/P